THE
SOUL
OF
ROCK 'N ROLL

THE
SOUL
OF
ROCK 'N ROLL

A History of African Americans in Rock Music

By J. Othello

REGENT PRESS
OAKLAND, CA.

ISBN: 1-58790-105-6

Library of Congress Control Number: 2004096468

Book and cover design: roz abraham, Regent Press
Contributing editor: j.t. hilliard

REGENT PRESS
6020–A Adeline Street
Oakland, CA 94608
www.regentpress.net

TABLE OF CONTENTS

INTRODUCTION

It's been said that the Soul Of Rock 'N Roll is a "damned" soul, invoking the legend of Robert Johnson and Mississippi Delta Blues Musicians going down to the crossroads to barter their eternal souls for musical fortune and fame.

Well, it wasn't the crossroads; it was more like the recording studio/office of some small-time record executive, or fast talkin' wax-merchant, purchasing the musical soul of some struggling Black bluesman for crumbs on the dollar. No residuals, no mechanicals, and no publishing royalties were paid, just a few dollars and the promise of more crumbs for the next piece of the songwriter's soul.

But then, to add insult to injury, "good folk" began shunning the sound and calling the original Black recordings "Race Music". To a greater degree, many in American society had even harsher names for the sound; calling the songs "Nigger Music", "Jungle Music", and many other names meant to insult and degrade the Black musicians and songwriters who created it. Some in America even went as far as to invoke an anti-religious label, calling it "The Devil's Music!"

Though the sound was called by many names, it always had the same effect on those who loved it; the music made folk want to move, clap, dance, shake, shout, strut, grind, rock and roll. It was the sound of a long day and a late night, and the feeling of cool hands on a hot body.

Blues enthusiast of the 1940s used the words "rock" and "roll", as being synonymous with sex. This was nothing new, since bop, swing and jazz, originally meant the same thing. So when Cleveland disc jockey Alan Freed began playing some of the more commercial sounding Black rhythm and blues "Race Records", he applied the old term "Rock and Roll," to now mean "Music with a raw and heavy backbeat". Freed did this to expand his audience to include white teenagers who loved the "Rhythm and Blues" sound. All of this, of course, resulting in feelings of displeasure and open protest from White parents and good church goin' folk. (source: mjet.com)

However, as soon as large American recording corporations saw that millions of dollars could be made from "Race Records", the American entrepreneurial spirit saw past the dark cloud of social resistance, and into the silver lining of profit. Black songs got a shiny White makeover. The recording corporations enlisted armies of White singers to re-record these unacceptable Black songs, and remake them into totally acceptable American Pop Standards.

So, it came as no surprise when, in the mid 1960s, (during the Civil Rights movement) the American recording corporations deemed it necessary to take the name "Rock and Roll" away from the Black musicians that created it, and dub Black music with a strong backbeat, "Rhythm and Blues" (R&B).

"Well I'll be damned!"

This is a history of African Americans in Rock Music, and how these beautiful musicians, and singers, impacted multicultural awareness, civil rights activism, social-economic improvement, social-academic achievement, and changed the face of music in the 20th Century, by creating and inspiring a completely original American art form...

Rock 'N Roll!

the

'50s

In the 1950s, African American musicians, in the process of creating Rock 'N Roll, had a profoundly positive impact on the level and scope of Multicultural Awareness in American society.

The invention of television, and the featuring of well-groomed, expensively clothed, extremely talented, and highly professional African American performers on TV and in films, helped the American public to discover a new and empowering image of Black people and Black Culture.

Consequently, artists like Chuck Berry, Little Richard, and Ike & Tina Turner set the style and the performance standards for the next 50 years of rock music.

CHUCK BERRY

(Born: October 18, 1926, St. Louis, Missouri)

Born Charles Edward Anderson Berry to a large family in St. Louis, Missouri, Chuck Berry was an exceptionally bright child, who enjoyed music, poetry, and had a deep and passionate love of the blues. When Chuck was a teenager, he won a high school talent contest and soon after began working the East St. Louis club scene. Chuck quickly found that Black audiences liked a variety of music, and really liked the sight of a Black man playing White hillbilly music. Consequently, Chuck's showmanship and super rockin' guitar playing skill quickly made him a favorite on the local scene.

In 1954, the Chuck Berry Trio and Ike Turner's Kings of Rhythm were the top acts in the Black community, but Chuck had bigger ideas; he wanted to record records. In 1955, Muddy Waters encouraged Chuck Berry to contact Chess Records. After listening to Chuck's demo tape, label president Leonard Chess scheduled a recording session, and signed Chuck to his label. Chess liked Chuck's song "Ida Red", and during the recording session the title was changed to "Maybellene".

"Maybellene" made it to the mid-'20s on the pop chart, and its overall influence was tremendous. Chuck Berry had a Black rock & roll record with broad appeal, and was embraced by White teenagers and southern musicians like Elvis Presley and Jerry Lee Lewis. Chuck quickly became famous for his blazing 24-bar guitar solos and his imaginative lyrics.

DJ Alan Freed helped get the record to a White teenage audience, and was given part of the writing credit by Chess as payment. Alan Freed was the first White DJ to use Chuck Berry on his rock & roll stage show at the Paramount and Brooklyn Fox theaters, which played to young White audiences. Also, when Hollywood came calling, Alan Freed made sure that Chuck appeared with him in the films "Rock! Rock! Rock!", "Go, Johnny, Go!", and "Mister Rock 'N Roll".

Within a year, Chuck Berry had gone from St. Louis and $15 a night, to Hollywood and $1,500 a night. In addition, Chuck started scoring hits with "Roll Over Beethoven", "Thirty Days", "Too Much Monkey Business", "Brown Eyed Handsome Man", "You Can't Catch Me", "School Day", "Carol", "Back in the U.S.A.", "Little Queenie", "Memphis, Tennessee", "Rock and Roll Music", and his signature "Johnny B. Goode".

Chuck was in constant demand, touring the country on racially mixed package shows, and appearing on television and in movies. In 1958, Chuck invested heavily in St. Louis area real estate and opened up a racially mixed nightspot called the Club Bandstand. Chuck Berry was an entrepreneur, and was making plans to open an amusement park in nearby Wentzville. However, when the St. Louis authorities found out that one of Chuck's hatcheck girls was also a prostitute, Chuck was charged with transporting a minor over state lines for the purpose of having sex. He had two trials, and was sentenced to two years in federal prison.

Chuck Berry emerged from prison bitter, but two things happened while Chuck was behind bars; British teenagers had discovered his music and were making his songs hits all over again, and American teenagers had discovered the Beatles and the Rolling Stones, who based their music on Chuck's style. Astonishingly, Chuck found himself in the middle of a worldwide phenomenon, with his music taking center stage.

Inspired by all of the respect and admiration, Chuck Berry came back with a vengeance, scoring the hits "Nadine," "No Particular Place to Go," and "You Never Can Tell". He toured Britain, and appeared on the big screen with his British disciples in the groundbreaking T.A.M.I. Show in 1964. Chuck Berry had found a new youthful audience who adored and worshiped him. In the late '60s, Chuck's live act included slow blues and quickly became a fixture on the festival and hippie ballroom circuit. In the early '70s, Chuck Berry scored his last hit with a live version of the semi-obscene, "My Ding a Ling," yielding Chuck his first official gold record.

By the end of the '70s, Chuck was as in demand everywhere, and worked every revival show, TV special and festival that he could. But again, in 1979, Chuck headed back to prison for income tax evasion. Upon his release, he appeared as himself in the Alan Freed biography, American Hot Wax, and was inducted into the Rock & Roll Hall of Fame. But Chuck refused to record any new material or issue a live album, and his live performances became increasingly fickle. This began to tarnish his reputation.

In 1987, he published his book, *Chuck Berry: The Autobiography*, and that same year the film documentary "Hail! Hail! Rock 'N Roll" was released, which included live footage from Chuck's 60th birthday concert. The Rolling Stones' Keith Richards was musical director, and many other music superstars came to honor Chuck.

When you think of the early days of Rock 'N Roll, only a few faces come to mind, and the one playing the guitar is Chuck Berry. To this day, Chuck's prolific catalog of unmistakable music and his legions of loyal fans endure. Chuck Berry has always been, and will always be, a Rock 'N Roll Original and Legend.

(sources: rollingstone.com, theiceberg.com, livedaily.citysearch.com)

LITTLE RICHARD

(Born: December, 5, 1935, Macon, Georgia)

Born Richard Wayne Penniman in Macon, Georgia, Little Richard was one of twelve children who grew up impoverished in the Deep South. When Richard was young, listening to the blues, country music, and gospel was a way of life in the Black community, and he learned to play piano from a flamboyant performer named Esquerita, who recorded rock 'n roll for Capitol Records.

In 1951, Richard first recorded the blues for RCA Records in Atlanta, with Billy Wright's Orchestra. "Taxi Blues" was the first of four unsuccessful single releases on the label. In 1953, Richard moved to Houston, Texas, with the Tempo Toppers and the Deuces of Rhythm, where he recorded four R&B singles including "Ain't That Good News". Eight months later he recorded another four songs with the Johnny Otis' Orchestra.

In February 1955, Richard sent a demo to Specialty Records, and later that same year, he would begin to make his mark in rock 'n roll at Specialty Records. Working with producer "Bumps" Blackwell at Cosimo Matassa's J&M Studio in New Orleans, Richard recorded a stunning succession of rock 'n roll hits over the next several years. Richard recorded a dozen tracks in New Orleans, including "Tutti Frutti", which gave him his first R&B and pop hit. Also, "Long Tall Sally", which topped the R&B chart and was the first of his three US Top 10 hits, despite being covered by Pat Boone, whose previous record, a cover version of "Tutti Frutti", was still charting. Richard's string of Top 20 hits continued with the double-sided "Rip It Up" his first UK release and chart entry in late 1956, and "Ready Teddy". Richard's unrestrained performance of "Long Tall Sally" and "Tutti Frutti", in the film "Don't Knock The Rock", helped to push his UK single to number three on the charts.

In 1957, Richard's next film and singles were "The Girl Can't Help It", along with the B-side "She's Got It", these gave him two more UK Top 20 hits. Richard scored three more huge transatlantic hits with "Lucille", "Keep A Knockin'", and "Jenny Jenny", featured in the Alan Freed movie "Mr. Rock & Roll". Richard also scored a Top 20 album with "Here's Little Richard". However, at the height of his young career, Richard shocked the rock world during an Australian tour, and announced that he was quitting music to go to a theological college.

In 1958, despite Richard's absence from the rock scene, previously recorded material such as the transatlantic Top 10 hit "Good Golly Miss Molly" kept his name on the chart. Also, a year later he had his biggest UK hit with a 1956 recording of "Baby Face", which reached number two on the charts.

Between 1958 and 1962, Richard recorded only gospel music for Gone, Mercury Records with producer Quincy Jones, and Atlantic Records. But in late 1962, Little Richard toured the UK for the first time and the wild man who pounded pianos and pierced eardrums returned to playing rock 'n roll with huge and triumphant success.

In 1963, Richard worked in Europe with the Beatles and the Rolling Stones, who were both great admirers of his music. Richard's first rock recordings of the 1960s were made back at Specialty Records and resulted in the UK top 20 hit "Bama Lama Bama Loo".

In 1964, Little Richard signed with Vee-Jay Records where he re-recorded all of his hits, revived a few oldies and cut some new songs; however, his sales were unimpressive. In the mid 1960s, soul music was taking over and Richard's soulful Vee Jay tracks, "I Don't Know What You've Got But It's Got Me", which featured a young Jimi Hendrix on guitar, and "Without Love", were among the best recordings of the times. For the rest of the 1960s, Little Richard continued to draw big crowds by singing his old hits.

In 1965, Richard mixed 50s rock and 60s soul for Modern Records. In 1966, he did the same at OKeh Records, and at Brunswick Records in 1967. The best of these were his OKeh tracks, which included "Poor Dog", "Hurry Sundown" and the UK-recorded "Get Down With It", which gave the group "Slade" their first hit in the 70s.

In 1970, Reprise Records tried very hard to return Little Richard to the top. Under the expertise of producer Richard Perry, he managed minor US hits with "Freedom Blues" and "Greenwood, Mississippi", but his three albums sold poorly. The rest of the 70s were spent jumping from label to label, and playing oldies shows. When Little Richard wanted to rock, he did, but there was often too much Las Vegas glitter, and excessive posturing. So, feeling unfulfilled, Richard returned to the ministry in 1976, and for the next decade preached throughout America.

In 1986, Richard was one of the first artists inducted into the Rock And Roll Hall of Fame and he successfully acted in the movie "Down And Out In Beverly Hills", stealing scenes from actors Nick Nolte, Bette Midler and Richard Dryfus. The film also included Little Richard performing a rocking version of "Great Gosh A'Mighty", which almost made the US Top 40. Renewed interest spurred WEA Records to sign him and release the album "Lifetime Friend".

Since the 1980s, Little Richard has become a frequent visitor on talk shows, and an in-demand guest on other artist's records. He has his own star on the Hollywood Walk of Fame and a boulevard named after him in his hometown of Macon. In the 1990s Little Richard released a series of rock'n nursery rhymes, children's songs, and children's videos; endearing him to a whole new generation of young fans. The artist, who shook up the music business and the parents of the 1950s, is now a beloved personality accepted by all age groups.

The wildest and arguably the greatest and most influential of all rock 'n roll singers and songwriters, Little Richard claims to be the architect of rock and roll. One thing is certain, his explosive music, charismatic persona, incredible piano playing and eternally mimicked vocals made Little Richard Penniman a Rock 'N Roll Legend.

(sources: rockabilly.net, littlerichard.com, rollingstone.com, theiceberg.com)

BIG MAMA THORNTON

(Born: December 11, 1926, Montgomery, Alabama)

Born Willie Mae Thornton in Montgomery, Alabama, she was one of seven children. Willie Mae's father was a minister, her mother sang in the church choir, and it was the church's early musical influences that helped Willie Mae win first place in an amateur singing show. Sammy Green of Atlanta saw her perform, and she went on to play with his "Hot Harlem Review."

In 1948 she moved to Houston, Texas, where she lived for a few years while she sang and wrote songs for performances in the local clubs. Willie Mae, Little Esther, and Mel Walker were a package show for Johnny Otis in the early 1950s. They became well known and went to New York to play the Apollo Theatre in 1952. Willie Mae sang the Dominoe's hit "Have Mercy Baby," and was a huge success, headlining the show the very next night at the Apollo. The nickname "Big Mama" was given to her after that first show, and it stuck. She was a large woman, and the name fit well with her barrel house vocal style.

In 1951, Don Robey signed her to Peacock Records, and in 1953, she flew from Houston to New York for the "Hound Dog" sessions. Jerry Lieber and Mike Stoller wrote "Hound Dog", and Willie Mae recorded it. The B-side was "They Call Me Big Mama," and the single sold almost two million copies. "Hound Dog" held down the top slot on Billboard's R&B charts for seven long weeks in 1953, and Elvis Presley went on to make "Hound Dog" a rock and roll classic three years later. Ironically, Willie Mae only received one $500 check for

"Hound Dog" in her entire life. In a similar occurrence, she wrote and recorded the hit song "Ball and Chain", which also later became a huge hit for Janis Joplin in the late 1960s.

Willie Mae left Houston in the early 1960s and moved to the San Francisco Bay area. She toured with shows in America and Europe, and played the Monterey Jazz Festival throughout the 1960s and 1970s. Willie Mae's style captured the attention of many fans through the years because she was beautiful, crazy, and wild, yet controlled in her singing. Many companies recorded her work, such as Arhoolie Records, who released Big Mama Thornton in Europe in 1966, and Big Mama Thornton with the Chicago Blues Band in 1967 with Muddy Waters, Lightnin' Hopkins, and Otis Spawn. In 1968, Ball and Chain compiled blues songs featuring Willie Mae.

In the early 1970s she recorded "Saved" for Pentagram Records and "She's Back" for the Backbeat Label. Vanguard Records recorded her twice before prison audiences in two penitentiaries with "Jail" and again with "Sassy Mama!" Willie Mae appeared in New York in 1983 at the Newport Jazz Festival with Muddy Waters, B.B. King, and Eddie Cleanhead Vinson. The show was recorded by Buddha records for the album, "The Blues-A Real Summit Meeting".

Willie Mae Thornton died in Los Angeles, California, of a heart attack, on July 25, 1984. Her last recording was released after her death by Ace Records in the UK on the album "Quit Snoopin' 'round My Door", and later that year she was inducted into the Blues Foundation's Hall of Fame.

Willie Mae "Big Mama" Thornton made a mighty mark on the music world with her powerful vocal sound and unforgettable style. To anybody who knows anything about music, Willie Mae "Big Mama" Thornton will always be remembered and revered as a Rock 'N Roll Hero and Legend.

(sources: roadhouseblues.com, rollingstone.com, theiceberg.com, VH1.com)

MUDDY WATERS

(Born: April 4, 1915, Rolling Fork, Mississippi)

Born McKinley Morganfield in Rolling Fork, Mississippi, Muddy Waters was one of the most dominant figures of post-World War II blues. He was raised in the rural Mississippi town of Clarksdale, were he began performing in juke joints, dives and various nightspots.

Muddy Waters toured the south making field recordings between 1941 and 1942. The following year he moved to Chicago, and began using electric instruments. By 1948, Muddy had signed a recording contract with the newly founded Aristocrat label, which later became Chess Records. Muddy's second release, "I Feel Like Goin' Home/I Can't Be Satisfied", was a minor R&B hit and set a pattern for several further singles, including "Rollin' And Tumblin'", "Rollin' Stone" and "Walking Blues".

By 1951 Muddy Waters was using a full backing band, and the Muddy Waters Band was Chicago's most influential unit, with recordings like "Hoochie Coochie Man", "I've Got My Mojo Working", "Mannish Boy", "You Need Love" and "I'm Ready". Muddy Waters' international stature was secured in 1958 when he toured Britain, and although he was criticized by some blues purists for his use of amplification, the overwhelming effect on a new generation of younger White fans was enormous.

However, in the wake of hip new '60s soul music, Muddy Waters' sound was deemed old-fashioned and he felt obliged to update his sound and repertoire. This resulted in such releases as "Electric

Mud", which featured a reading of the Rolling Stones' classic "Let's Spend The Night Together", but his work during the 1960s was disappointing. "The London Sessions" kept him in the public eye, as did his appearance in the film, "The Last Waltz", but it was an inspired series of collaborations with guitarist Johnny Winter that signaled a dramatic rebirth for Muddy. Johnny Winter produced and arranged four excellent albums that recaptured the fire of Muddy Waters' early releases and conferred a sense of dignity to Muddy Waters' musical legacy.

Muddy Waters died of heart failure in 1983. He is considered one of the world's most important, influential and inspiring musicians, and a bonafide Rock 'N Roll Legend!

(sources: muddywaters.com, motorcityblues.com, rollingstone.com, VH1.com)

B.B. KING

(Born: September 16, 1925, Itta Bena, Mississippi)

Born Riley B. King in Itta Bena, Mississippi, his childhood was not easy, and young Riley (B.B.) was shuttled between his mother and his grandmother. Young Riley put in long days working as a sharecropper and sang in church before moving to Indianola, Mississippi, in 1943.

B.B. King loved country and gospel music, but was mostly influenced by the blues of T-Bone Walker and Lonnie Johnson, and the jazz of Charlie Christian and Django Reinhardt. In 1946, young Riley (B.B.) set off for Memphis, Tennessee, to look up his cousin, country blues guitarist Bukka White. For almost a year, Bukka taught Riley (B.B.) the blues guitar.

After returning briefly to Indianola, Riley (B.B.) returned to Memphis again in 1948. He was soon performing and broadcasting live via Memphis radio station WDIA, the station had recently switched to an all-Black format. Local club owners wanted their musicians to have radio gigs so they could plug their nightly appearances at the club. At first, young Riley King called himself "The Peptikon Boy" after an alcoholic drink, but when WDIA put him on the air, his on-air name became the "Beale Street Blues Boy," later shortened to Blues Boy, and finally the now legendary "B.B. King".

In 1949, the newly named B.B. King recorded his first four tracks for Bullet Records, and signed a record contract with RPM Records in Los Angeles. He recorded prolifically in Memphis over the next couple of years. Many of his early recordings were produced by the now legendary Sam Phillips, later of Sun Records. Sam Phillips was independently producing sides for both RPM and Chess Records, with artists including Howlin' Wolf, and Rosco Gordon.

In 1951, B.B. King had his first national R&B hit with "Three O'Clock Blues", previously recorded by Lowell Fulson. B.B. King's Memphis contemporaries included vocalist Bobby Bland, drummer Earl Forest, and singer and pianist Johnny Ace. When B.B. King hit the road to promote "Three O'Clock Blues," he handed his group, the Beale Streeters, over to Johnny Ace.

It was during this time that B.B. King first named his guitar "Lucille". The story goes: while he was playing a show in Twist, Arkansas, a fight broke out between two men over a woman. The brawlers knocked over a garbage pail filled with kerosene used to heat the place, and set the room on fire. In the rush to escape the flames, B.B. King left his guitar inside. Then, realizing he had left his instrument, he ran back in, dodging the flames and almost losing his life. When the fire was over, he learned that the lady whom the fight started over was named Lucille. Plenty of 'Lucilles' have passed through his hands since then, but the original was born by fire.

In the 1950s, B.B. King recorded mostly in L.A and he scored 20 hits, including, "You Know I Love You" in 1952, "Woke Up This Morning" and "Please Love Me" in 1953, "When My Heart Beats like a Hammer", "Whole Lotta' Love", and "You Upset Me Baby" in 1954, "Every Day I Have the Blues", "Sneakin' Around", and "Ten Long Years" in 1955, "Bad Luck", "Sweet Little Angel", and "On My Word of Honor" in 1956, and "Please Accept My Love" in 1958. Reflectively, B.B. King and his guitar were influencing a legion of young players across the nation, and eventually around the world.

In 1960, B.B. King recordings of "Sweet Sixteen", "Got a Right to Love My Baby" and "Partin' Time", became hits. In 1962, he moved over to ABC-Paramount Records following the lead of Ray Charles, and Fats Domino, and in 1964, B.B. King recorded his "Live at the Regal" album at the Chicago theater. That same year, he enjoyed a minor hit with "How Blue Can You Get". His recordings of "Don't Answer the Door" and "Paying the Cost to Be the Boss" were top ten R&B singles in 1966, and "Why I Sing the Blues" was a hit in 1969.

In 1969, super-stardom finally arrived for B.B. King, when he crossed-over to the mainstream with his biggest hit, "The Thrill Is Gone". Roy Hawkins' wrote the violin-laidened minor-key master-piece, which was a unique departure from the horn-powered arrangements B.B. King normally used. Not only was the track a number three R&B hit, but it was a hit on the pop charts as well.

B.B. King was one of only a few bluesmen to score hits consistently during the 1970s. In 1973, he went to Philadelphia and recorded "To Know You Is to Love You" and "I Like to Live the Love", with the same rhythm section that recorded hits with the Spinners and the O'Jays. Both songs were huge sellers, and in 1976, he teamed up with his old friend Bobby Bland and recorded some well-received duets. In 1978, he joined forces with the Crusaders to record "Never Make Your Move Too Soon" and "When It All Comes Down".

B.B. King was a road warrior who used to gig an average of 300 nights a year. His 1993 MCA album "Blues Summit", with his peers John Lee Hooker, Etta James, Lowell Fulson, and Koko Taylor, was a big success. In 1999, B.B. King recorded "Let the Good Times Roll: The Music of Louis Jordan", and in 2000, he recorded "Riding With The King", a collaboration with English rock legend Eric Clapton.

B.B. King's internationally recognizable guitar style and trademark sound set him apart from his contemporaries. Add his patented plead-ing vocal style and B.B. King is arguably one of the most influential bluesman in American history, and hands down, a Rock 'N Roll Legend in his own time.

(sources: rhythmandtheblues.org, rollingstone.com, VH1.com, theiceberg.com, livedaily.citysearch.com)

BO DIDDLEY

(Born: December, 28, 1928, McComb, Mississippi)

Born Otha Ellas McDaniel in the small town of McComb, Mississippi, Bo moved with his family to Chicago at age eight. Bo got his first guitar from his sister, and found his way to the blues when he heard John Lee Hooker in a Chicago nightclub. Bo Diddley was a nickname given him when he was a Golden Glove boxer. Bo was tough, and while most of the era's songs were fun and upbeat, Bo Diddley's lyrics were dark and ominous. His music was powered by his signature rhythm that echoed inside your skull, and rocked you to the bone.

In late 1954, he recorded demos of "I'm A Man" and "Bo Diddley", and re-recorded at Chess Studios, "Bo Diddley", became a R&B hit in 1955. Before long, Bo Diddley's distorted, amplified, custom-made guitar, with its rectangular shape and pumping rhythm style became a familiar, much-imitated trademark, as did his self-referring songs with titles like "Bo Diddley's A Gunslinger", "Diddley Daddy" and "Bo's A Lumberjack". In 1959, "Say Man" was a US Top 20 hit, and "Pretty Thing" and "Hey Good Lookin'", reached the UK charts in 1963. Bo Diddley was regarded as a R&B legend and found international popularity, courtesy of the UK Rock 'N Roll boom. The Rolling Stones, the Animals, Manfred Mann, the Kinks, and the Yardbirds covered Bo's songs with great success.

In the 1960s, Bo Diddley played on albums by Chuck Berry and Muddy Waters, and appeared at large rock 'n roll festivals. His classic version of "Who Do You Love" became a staple cover for a new generation of US acts ranging from the Doors to Bob Seger. Like many of his generation, Bo Diddley attempted to update his image, and in the 1970s released "The Black Gladiator" and "Where It All Begins", produced by Johnny Otis.

In 1979, Bo toured with punk rock legends The Clash, and in 1983 took a role in the movie Trading Places with Eddie Murphy and Dan Ackroyd. In 1995, Bo Diddley signed with Code Blue records, and recorded the album, "A Man Amongst Men".

Bo Diddley is considered one of the founding fathers of rock 'n roll, his hypnotic beats, his vast array of electric custom-built guitars, use of reverb, tremolo and distortion, use of female musicians, and wild stage shows, pre-date all others. Bo Diddley was inducted into the Rock 'n Roll Hall of Fame in 1987, and in 1998 received a Lifetime Achievement Award at the Grammy Awards Ceremony. Bo Diddley played a crucial role in the history of rock 'n roll during his 40-year career. Bo Diddley is regarded as a legendary figure in the history of rock 'n roll, his sound and signature rhythm continues to remain an enormous influence on rock music. If you've ever heard the songs "I Want Candy", Buddy Holly's "Not Fade Away", or George Michael's "Faith", then you've heard the Bo Diddley rhythm, one of the most famous guitar rhythms in Rock 'N Roll History. Bo Diddley's undeniable influence, stamina, and pure hard-edged attitude make Bo Diddley an undisputed Rock 'N Roll Legend!

(sources: bandhunt.com, rockintown.com, bayblues.org, theiceberg.com)

JOHN LEE HOOKER

(Born: Aug. 17, 1920, Clarksdale, Mississippi)

John Lee Hooker was born in Clarksdale, Mississippi, and grew up singing spirituals, and the blues. John Lee's stepfather was bluesman Will Moore, and Moore's friends were legends like Blind Lemon Jefferson, Charley Patton, and Blind Blake. These individuals indelibly impressed young John Lee Hooker.

John Lee went to Memphis while he was still in his teens, but he wasn't very successful. So he relocated to Cincinnati, Ohio, where he sang in such gospel groups as the Fairfield Four and the Big Six. He lived in Cincinnati for seven years before moving to Detroit, Michigan, in 1943. In Detroit, John Lee drifted from day gig to day gig, and at night he played the blues. A club scene along Hastings Street was growing, and what he saw and heard inspired young John Lee Hooker.

In 1948, John Lee began working with entrepreneur Bernie Besman, who helped him release his solo debut, "Sally Mae" and "Boogie Chillen". John Lee's dark, reflective vocals were backed only by his heavily amplified guitar and constantly pounding foot. Modern Records in Los Angeles released the singles, and "Boogie Chillen" went to the top of the R&B charts. In 1949, Modern Records released several more major hits by John Lee, including, "Hobo Blues", "Hoogie Boogie", and "Crawling King Snake Blues". In 1951, John Lee topped the charts with "I'm in the Mood", where he overdubbed his voice three times, in an early attempt at multi-tracking.

John Lee Hooker made a prolific amount of recordings for a

multitude of record labels. Remarkably, and with question of ethical legality, John Lee did this all at the same time. Along with Modern records, John Lee Hooker recorded for King Records as Texas Slim, Regent Records as Delta John, Savoy Records as Birmingham Sam and his Magic Guitar, Danceland Records as Little Pork Chops, and Staff Records as Johnny Williams. John Lee also recorded for Sensation Records, and scored a national hit in 1950 with "Huckle Up, Baby". Further, John Lee recorded for Gotham Records, Regal Records, Swing Time Records, Federal Records, and Gone Records as John Lee Booker. But there's more! John Lee recorded with Chess Records, and Acorn Records as the Boogie Man, and Chance Records and DeLuxe Records as Johnny Lee. John Lee Hooker recorded with all of those record labels, including, JVB Records, Chart Records and Specialty Records, before finally settling down at Vee-Jay Records in 1955 under his own name.

John Lee Hooker became the personification of the growing Detroit blues scene during this incredibly prolific period. In 1955, Vee-Jay Records adapted John Lee Hooker to a band format. John Lee had worked with various bands over the years, but never with sidemen as talented as guitarist Eddie Taylor and harmonica player Jimmy Reed, who backed John Lee on the sessions that produced "Time Is Marching" and "Mambo Chillun". In 1956, John Lee and Eddie Taylor worked together on the session that recorded the John Lee Hooker classics, "Baby Lee" and "Dimples". In Addition, Taylor anchored the rhythm section when John Lee made it back to the R&B charts with "I Love You Honey" in 1958.

In 1960, Vee-Jay presented John Lee Hooker in an array of settings, and "No Shoes" was a hit, and in 1962, the single "Boom Boom" was his top seller. "Boom Boom" was a R&B dance number that crossed-over to pop radio, benefiting from the presence of some Motown house musicians. John Lee also recorded acoustic tracks aimed at the burgeoning folk-blues crowd, as well as some attempts at R&B that featured female background vocals.

Now legendary British blues bands such as the Animals and Yardbirds idolized John Lee Hooker during the early '60s, and their covers of his songs even out sold John Lee's original recordings. John Lee Hooker visited Europe in 1962 for the first American Folk Blues Festival, and recorded the popular records "Let's Make It" and "Shake It Baby" for European fans. In 1964, John Lee Hooker recorded his last hit for Vee-Jay, "Big Legs, Tight Skirt". Many considered it one of his best efforts, before setting off on another extended round of label hopping. In 1965 and 1966, John Lee recorded albums for Verve-Folkways Records, Impulse Records, Chess Records, and BluesWay Records.

In 1970, John Lee Hooker's reputation among the hip rock crowd grew after he teamed up with rockers Canned Heat for the massive selling album "Hooker 'n Heat". Nevertheless, in the late '70s the boogie formula fell momentarily out of style, and many of John Lee's recordings from that era found him just collaborating with rock rhythm sections, and getting very little attention. For John Lee Hooker, the Disco era sucked!

However, in 1980, A cameo appearance in the now legendary movie "The Blues Brothers", introduced John Lee Hooker to a new generation of blues enthusiasts. Feeling rejuvenated, John Lee enlisted producer and slide guitarist Roy Rogers to record "The Healer", with guest stars Carlos Santana, Bonnie Raitt, and Robert Cray, and "The Healer" won John Lee Hooker a well-deserved Grammy Award. Point-blank Records signed John Lee Hooker, and releasing "Mr. Lucky", with stars like Albert Collins, John Hammond, Van Morrison and Keith Richards accompanying him. This album was also a great success.

John Lee Hooker was inducted into the Rock 'N Roll Hall of Fame in 1991, and later in the decade opened a blues club in San Francisco called "John Lee Hooker's Boom Boom Room". On a given night you could enter the club and find John Lee sitting smoothly in his red velvet reserved booth, surrounded by bright-eyed admirers, and enjoying his beloved blues. Quietly, on June 21, 2001, the prolific John Lee

Hooker died at age 83, in his home near San Francisco, California. He was beloved worldwide as the king of the endless boogie, and a genuine Blues and Rock 'N Roll Legend.

(sources: theiceberg.com, livedaily.citysearch.com, rollingstone.com, VH1.com, rhythmandtheblues.org)

RAY CHARLES

(Born: September, 23, 1930, Albany, Georgia)

Ray Charles Robinson was born into a poor family in Albany, Georgia. Young Ray contracted glaucoma at the age of 5 and was completely blind by age 7. Ray studied music and Braille at the St. Augustine School for the Deaf and Blind in Florida. While enrolled in the St. Augustine School, he learned and became familiar with many musical instruments. One of the nicknames Ray would pick up was "The Genius", because when young Ray discovered that mathematics correlated to music, he began writing and arranging music in his head.

Following the death of Ray's mother in 1946, young Ray left St. Augustine's and traveled throughout the South with a variety of bands, playing saxophone, clarinet, and piano. He moved to Seattle, Washington, in 1948, where he formed the McSon Trio. They became the first Black performers to have a fully sponsored television show in the Northwest. It was also in Seattle that Ray met a young Quincy Jones, and marked the start of a lifelong friendship. It was around this time, that Ray dropped Robinson from his stage name, so he would not be mistaken for boxer "Sugar" Ray Robinson.

In 1950, Ray Charles began his professional recording career when he moved to Los Angeles. While Ray was signed to the Swingtime record label he scored two top ten hits. In 1952, Ray was signed to Atlantic Records, and it was during this time that Ray also played and arranged for blues and R&B legends such as Guitar Slim, Lowell

Fulson, and Ruth Brown. In 1954, Ray Charles formed his own band and began fusing different styles of music. Ray melodically melded gospel, jazz, and blues, and this fusion is credited by many as influencing the early sound of rock 'n roll. Ray Charles is also often credited with creating modern "soul music". In 1955, Ray Charles scored his first number one hit on the R&B charts, with "I've Got A Woman". Ray's fourth R&B number one, "What I'd Say," cracked the pop top ten, and in the summer of 1959, it reached number six.

In 1960, Ray Charles signed to the ABC-Paramount label and began to reach an even wider audience. His ABC-Paramount era hits began with the classic single, "Georgia On My Mind", his first pop-chart number one. 1960 also marked the first time Ray reached the top 10 with one of his albums, "The Genius Hits The Road". In 1961, Ray's crossover success earned him his first four Grammys, including two awards for his vocal performance on "Georgia," and a Best Album Vocal Performance award for "The Genius of Ray Charles". More hits followed that year, including the jazz/soul instrumental "One Mint Julep", which reached number one on the R&B charts, and number eight on the pop charts. Ray also had a top five album with "Genius + Soul = Jazz", and the R&B and pop chart smash "Hit The Road Jack".

In 1962, Ray began the year at the top of the R&B charts with "Unchain My Heart". This was Ray Charles' most successful year ever, and his next release was "Modern Sounds In Country and Western Music", an album with pop, country and blues overtones. This album spent 14 weeks at the top of Billboard's Top 200 chart, and produced the best-selling single on both the R&B, and the pop charts for that year. The single, "I Can't Stop Loving You" won a Grammy in 1963, and held the number one spot on the R&B chart for 10 weeks. Volume Two of the collection reached number two on the album charts, and the single, "You Are My Sunshine", gave Ray Charles his third R&B number one hit.

Also in 1963, Ray Charles received another Grammy Award for Best R&B Recording, for the single "Busted". Prophetically, Ray was arrested for heroin use, but never served any jail time. In 1965, Ray faced federal narcotics charges, and was forced to clean up, or go to prison. Ray's arrest and treatment interrupted his performing schedule, but he returned to music in 1966 with the hits "Crying Time", and his final R&B number one hit, the ironically titled, "Let's Go Get Stoned". Ray also contributed to the soundtracks for the films, "The Cincinnati Kid" in 1965, and "In The Heat of the Night" in 1967.

Ray Charles spent the rest of the 1960s and '70s touring relentlessly, and releasing at least one album per year. Ray made a cameo appearance in 1980s comedy classic movie "The Blues Brothers", which highlighted Ray's sense of humor. In 1982, Ray Charles was inducted into the Blues Hall of Fame, and in 1984, he made a successful return to country music with the album "Friendship", an album of duets with some of country music's biggest stars. In 1985, Ray performed on USA For Africa's recording of "We Are The World", and in 1990, Ray Charles was introduced to the 'Generation-X' crowd with his appearances in Diet Pepsi TV ads. Later that decade, in 1996, Ray released the album "Strong Love Affair" on long time friend Quincy Jones' Qwest/Warner Bros. label.

In 2002, Ray Charles released "Thanks For Bringing Love Around Again", which included a new version of his first big pop hit, "What I'd Say", and quietly, in 2004, "The Genius" Ray Charles passed away after a long and inspiring life.

Ray Charles was a legendary singer, songwriter, and pianist. His style of merging gospel, jazz, and the blues influenced generations of popular music performers and made Ray Charles a Rock 'N Roll Legend and Icon.

(sources: worldbook.com, grabow.biz, askmen.com, VH1.com, rollingstone.com, rhythmandtheblues.org)

IKE & TINA TURNER

Ike Turner was a rockstar long before he met Tina. In 1951, Ike Turner, and his Kings of Rhythm, scored a major hit with the single "Rocket 88". Ike recorded it at Sun Studios in Memphis while Elvis and Jerry Lee Lewis were still young teenagers, and this single is considered by many to be the first Rock 'n Roll record.

Ike Turner met Anna Mae Bullock in an East St. Louis club in the 1950s. Ike and Anna married, and Ms. Bullock became Tina Turner, a part time, and then full-time member of the band. For the recording of "A Fool In Love" the scheduled singer failed to appear and Tina filled in. When the song became a hit, Ike decided to make Tina the group's focal point. Through the 1950s and 1960s the Ike & Tina Revue scored several R&B hits and toured constantly.

In 1966, famed producer Phil Spector recorded the single "River Deep, Mountain High", a multi-tracked super production with orchestral arrangements topped by Tina's vocals. The single and the accompanying album were considered "overblown" for its time, but "River Deep, Mountain High" hit number 3 on the UK charts.

Ike & Tina's next phase was as an inspired covers act. They recorded C.C.R.'s "Proud Mary", the Rolling Stones' "Honky Tonk Women" and the Beatles' "Come Together". Tina's now legendary intro. on "Proud Mary" stands as one of the highlights of this phase, and Ike & Tina's own "Nutbush City Limits" was another hit track featuring Tina's hard-edged vocals.

In 1969, Ike & Tina went on tour with the Rolling Stones, giving Ike & Tina some well-deserved exposure. However, under the weight of constant touring, recording, family struggles, and an abusive dynamic between Ike and everyone, the whole thing ran out of steam in the early 1970s. A few years later Tina left Ike, and they were divorced.

In the late 1970s, Tina Turner embarked on a solo career, performing with a new backup band in small clubs. Her first album, "Rough" in 1978, didn't sell very well, prompting Tina to switch management to Roger Davies, who rebuilt her career by changing her image from R&B diva to "The Queen of Rock". Tina opened three shows for her old friends the Rolling Stones, and began her comeback.

Tina signed a deal with Capitol Records, and recorded the album "Private Dancer" in London. The album took less than two weeks to record, and produced the 1984 number one hit single "What's Love Got to Do With It?" The album went on to sell 10 million copies worldwide, making Tina Turner a superstar. That year Tina also made a memorable appearance with mega-actor Mel Gibson, starring in the film "Mad Max Beyond Thunderdome". Tina's work on the soundtrack produced the hit single, "We Don't Need Another Hero", and that next year, Tina won three Grammys and embarked on a successful world tour.

After a stunning appearance at Live Aid, Tina Turner returned in 1986 with the album, "Break Every Rule". The album was a top seller, and that same year Tina began dating German record executive Erwin Bach, with whom she lives to this day. Tina Turner's next albums, Foreign Affair in 1989, Simply the Best in 1991, and Wildest Dreams in 1996, sustained her status as an international superstar. Her autobiography, co-written with MTV's Kurt Loder, "I, Tina", inspired the 1993 Oscar-nominated movie "What's Love Got to Do with It". The Film chronicled Tina's version of life with Ike, and painted Ike Turner as a villainous tyrant, bully, misogynist, junky, and rapist. Dramatically, it served to fuel the rough singing, rough loving, rough living, legend of the Ike and Tina Turner relationship.

Tina Turner is a star in the states, but she is even bigger overseas, especially in Britain. At one point, Tina held the world record for largest paying audience attending a solo performance, performing to over 180,000 people in Brazil in 1988. Tina Turner has sold over 50 million albums worldwide, and was inducted into the Rock and Roll Hall of Fame in 1991.

Tina's album, "Twenty-Four Seven", was released in 2000, and ironically, as Tina's career rose, Ike's sank. Long-standing drug problems landed Ike in prison. Sadly, Ike Turner usually gets dismissed as Tina's abusive and tyrannical husband, or, is so overshadowed by Tina's success that he hardly seems worth mentioning. But, if it hadn't been for Ike Turner, there would be no Tina Turner. This fact makes them both, Rock 'N Roll Legends.

(sources: rockintown.com, rollingstone.com, theiceberg.com, VH1.com)

THE ISLEY BROTHERS

The first generation of Isley Brothers were born and raised in Cincinnati, Ohio, where they were encouraged to begin a singing career by their father, a professional vocalist, and their mother, a church pianist who provided musical accompaniment for their early performances. Initially a gospel quartet, the group was comprised of brothers O'Kelly, Ronald, Rudolph, and Vernon Isley. However, in 1955, Vernon Isley died in a bicycling accident, and the group became a trio, with Ronald Isley as the lead vocalist.

In 1957, the brothers went to New York City to record a string of doo-wop singles. Two years later in Washington, D.C., while performing a spirited performance of the song "Lonely Teardrops", they interjected the line "You know you make me want to shout", which caused an audience frenzy. An RCA executive saw the concert, and signed the Isleys soon after, insisting that their first single be "Shout!" Unfortunately, the single failed to reach the pop Top 40 on its initial release, but it eventually became a frequently covered classic.

In 1962, the brothers had a hit with "Twist and Shout". Like so many of the Isley Brothers' earlier R&B recordings, "Twist and Shout" earned greater commercial success when performed by White groups like the Beatles.

During a 1964 tour, The Isley Brothers recruited young guitarist Jimmy James to play in their backing band. Jimmy James later shot to fame under his given name, Jimi Hendrix. Jimi made his first recordings with the Isleys, including the single "Testify," issued on the Isley Brothers' own T-Neck label.

The Isley Brothers signed to the Motown Records subsidiary label Tamla in 1965, where they joined forces with the famed writing and production team Holland-Dozier-Holland. Their first single, the hit "This Old Heart of Mine" barely missed the pop top ten. It was their only hit on Motown, however, when the song hit number three in Britain in 1967, the Isleys relocated to England in order to sustain their career.

After years of writing their own material, the Isleys felt stifled by the Motown production formula, and by the time they returned stateside in 1969, they had exited Tamla to their own T-Neck label. Later that same year, they released the smash single "It's Your Thing", which hit number two on the U.S. charts, and became their most successful record. Also that year, younger brothers Ernie and Marvin Isley, neighbor Chris Jasper and family friend Everett Collins became The Isley Brothers' new backing band.

In the '70s, inspired by Ernie Isley's hard-edged guitar playing, the group began incorporating rock material into its repertoire, and scored hits with covers of Stephen Stills' "Love the One You're With", War's "Spill the Wine" and Bob Dylan's "Lay Lady Lay".

In 1973, the Isleys scored a massive hit with their rock-funk fusion version of their own "Who's That Lady", retitled "That Lady (Part I)", and the album "3 + 3" also proved highly successful, as did 1975s "The Heat Is On", which produced the hit single "Fight the Power (Part I)". In the latter '70s, the group again altered its sound to fit into the booming disco market, and frequently topped the R&B charts with singles like "Climbin' up the ladder", "Voyage to Atlantis", "Footsteps in the Dark", and "The Pride" in 1977. In 1978, they scored again with "Take Me to the Next Phase (Part 1)", "I Wanna Be With You (Part 1)" in 1979, and "Don't Say Goodnight" in 1980.

While the Isleys' popularity continued into the 1980s, Ernie, Marvin, and Chris Jasper, left the band in 1984 to form their own group,

Isley, Jasper, Isley, and they topped the R&B charts with "Caravan of Love" a year later.

Tragically, in 1986, O'Kelly Isley died of a heart attack. Soon after, Rudolph left the group to pursue his calling to the ministry. Although the individual members continued with solo work and side projects respectively, the Isley Brothers as a group would always forge on in one form or another. In the later part of the 1990s, Ronald Isley was featured in a series of now famous R.Kelly videos and duets, starring Ronald as the now legendary Mr. Biggs character, a smooth singing Godfather-type gangster for a new generation.

Collectively, The Isley Brothers have been one of the music industry's most prolific and best-loved groups, releasing over thirty albums, and countless singles. The Isley Brothers experienced a resurgence in 2001, and their album Eternal appeared on Top 10 Albums of the Year lists across the country. The Isleys continue making music into the new millennium, and consistently offer a host of great musical performances and collaborations.

The Isley Brothers enjoyed one of the longest, most influential and diverse careers in popular music. In six decades of performing, The Isley Brothers distinguished history has spanned not only two generations of Isley siblings but also epic cultural changes which inspired their music's transformation from gospel to doo-wop to R&B to soul to blistering rock and funk and back again. Without a doubt, The Isley Brothers are intrepid and enduring Rock 'N Roll Heroes.

(sources: rollingstone.com, VH1.com, theiceberg.com, livedaily.citysearch.com, abc.abcnews.go.com)

the

'60s

In the 1960s, African American Rock 'N Roll Artists contributed greatly to the Civil Rights movement and used their financial resources and celebrity to further the cause of social justice.

The image and names of highly respected Black music professionals like Aretha Franklin and James Brown, raised the national consciousness and shined a star bright light on the fight for social and racial equity.

ARETHA FRANKLIN

(Born March 25, 1942, Memphis, Tennessee)

Aretha Franklin was born into the home of the Reverend and Mrs. C.L. Franklin, who encouraged their daughters, Aretha, Carolyn and Erma, to sing. The three sisters sang in the church choir every Sunday, listening to the sermons of their father, a well-known Preacher and gospel singer, and fellowshipping with future stars like Smokey Robinson and Sam Cooke.

At age 15, Aretha became an unwed mother, and by age 17 she had two sons. In 1960, Aretha's grandmother took Aretha and her two children to New York, where she began recording demo tapes and attracting national attention for her singing talent. After declining offers from RCA and Motown, Aretha Franklin signed to Columbia Records; however, the Columbia years were confusing for Aretha, who was directed into pop music rather than R&B. Columbia was considered a White company that didn't appreciate her talent. The company produced 10 of her albums, but she had only one pop hit in six years with "Rock-a-bye Your Baby with a Dixie Melody".

In 1966, when her Columbia contract expired, producer Jerry Wexler signed her to Atlantic Records and returned Aretha to her R&B roots. In 1967, Jerry Wexler brought Aretha Franklin to the Florence Alabama Music Emporium studios in Muscle Shoals. There, Aretha recorded "I Never Loved a Man (the Way I Love You)", which was a hit sensation and convinced Aretha to finish the album in New York.

During the next three years, Aretha Franklin sold millions of albums with Top 20 crossover hits like "The House That Jack Built", "Baby I Love You", "Chain of Fools", "Since You've Been Gone", "Think", and her signature "Respect". The single "Respect" had a larger meaning during the era of black activism, feminism/womanism and sexual freedom. "Respect" won Aretha Franklin two Grammy awards and an honorary award from Dr. Martin Luther King Jr.

While famous and well respected, Aretha hid a personal life full of hardship from the world. In 1969, after she had her third son, her troubled eight-year marriage ended, and her father was arrested for possession of marijuana. But Aretha didn't allow her personal struggles to interfere with her music.

In the early 1970s, Aretha Franklin scored hits with "Bridge Over Troubled Water", "Don't Play That Song", "Spanish Harlem", "Rock Steady", and give birth to her fourth son. Between 1969 and 1975, Aretha Franklin won Grammy awards every year, and even sang at President Jimmy Carter's inauguration. However, by the end of the 1970s her record sales were beginning to decline.

In 1980, Aretha Franklin gave her career a boost with a cameo appearance in The Blues Brothers, and as it had done for many others, the movie introduced Aretha to a young audience of new and appreciative fans. That same year, she left Atlantic and signed with Arista Records, with whom she recorded hits like "Freeway of Love" and "Who's Zoomin' Who". Aretha's first Arista album, became her highest charting album since 1972. Tragically, in 1984, Aretha's father, The Reverend C.L. Franklin, died of gunshot wounds suffered during a robbery attempt at his home five years earlier. The Reverend C.L. Franklin was a highly respected and revered figure in the nation-wide Black community, and his influences and vision for his family will be felt for generations to come.

As the 1980s continued, Aretha won a Grammy Award for her number one single duet with George Michael, "I Knew You Were Waiting (For Me)", and in 1987, she won another Grammy Award for Best Soul Gospel Performance with "One Lord, One Faith, One Baptism".

That same year, Aretha Franklin became the first woman inducted into the Rock and Roll Hall of Fame. Enormous personal tragedy struck again in 1988, when her sister Carolyn died, as did Aretha's brother, and her personal manager. In grief and mourning, Aretha gracefully backed out of the spotlight for the remainder of that year.

In the 1990s, Aretha's reign continued. Along with a long list of accolades, a performance at President Bill Clinton's 1993 inauguration, an A&E Biography and countless television appearances, Aretha Franklin's legacy only became stronger. In 1998, Aretha released the critically acclaimed album, "A Rose Is Still a Rose", which featured production work by new generation superstars Lauryn Hill and Sean "P. Diddy" Combs.

Aretha Franklin is amazing! She has more than a dozen million-selling singles, 20 number one hits, a cover story in Time Magazine, a civil rights award from Martin Luther King, a spot in the Rock and Roll Hall of Fame, and 15 Grammys; including a lifetime achievement award in 1995. Her lifelong love of music, and her brilliant singing, created a legacy and Rock 'N Roll legend that is unmatched. She has overcome tremendous personal turmoil and tragedy, and has still risen to every occasion. This dedication to her art, and the adoration of millions of fans worldwide, makes Aretha Franklin the undisputed 'Queen of Soul', and an internationally "Respected" Rock 'N Roll Icon!

(sources: theiceberg.com, VH1.com, rollingstone.com, rhythmandtheblues.org)

SMOKEY ROBINSON

(Born: February 19, 1940, Detroit, Michigan)

Born William Robinson in Detroit, Michigan, this premier songwriter and performer, with more than 4,000 songs to his credit, formed his group the Miracles at Northern High School in 1955. It's been said that, except for Motown founder Berry Gordy, no single figure has been more closely associated with Detroit music than Smokey Robinson. In addition to leading his own group, the Miracles, Smokey was a producer, songwriter, talent scout and executive for Motown Records.

The Miracles began as the Matadors, a five-member harmony group whose songs were written by the teenage Smokey Robinson. In 1958, the renamed Miracles first single, "Got a Job" and "My Mama Done Told Me", was released on Smokey's 18th birthday. Over the course of his career at Motown, Smokey had a string of hit ballads sung in his signature falsetto, including "Ooh Baby Baby", "The Tracks of My Tears" and "The Tears of a Clown".

In early 1961, The Miracles' first hit, "Shop Around", sold more than a million copies, and rose to number two on the pop charts and number one on the R&B charts. Everything at Motown was in-house in those days. The Supremes, first known as the Primettes, wound up auditioning at Motown because Diana Ross was Smokey's neighbor, and the Primettes' guitarist, Marv Tarplin, became an accompanist, arranger, and co-writer of Smokey's.

Smokey's 27 Top Forty hits with the Miracles are only part of his accomplishments at Motown. Smokey also wrote and produced for many other Motown artists, including "Ain't That Peculiar", and "I'll Be Doggone" for Marvin Gaye, "Get Ready", "The Way You Do the Things You Do", and "My Girl" for The Temptations", "My Guy", and "You Beat Me to the Punch" for Mary Wells, and "Don't Mess With Bill", and "The Hunter Gets Captured by the Game" for the Marvelettes.

In 1972, Smokey parted ways with the Miracles, and enjoyed his biggest solo hits, "Cruisin'", and "Being With You", in the late '70s and early '80s. Smokey Robinson was a vice-president at Motown Records until the company's sale to MCA Records in 1988, and he left the label as an artist two years later. Notably, in his autobiography, Smokey revealed that he had been battling against cocaine addiction for many years, and although his marriage failed, he returned to full health creativity, and had two big hits in 1987 with, "Just To See Her" and "One Heartbeat".

In 1988, Smokey Robinson was inducted into the Rock And Roll Hall Of Fame, and returned to Motown Records in the late 1990s. Smokey Robinson is a legendary performer, writer and producer who will always be remembered for his outstanding work. Folk Legend Bob Dylan called Smokey Robinson "America's greatest living poet". This, along with his unforgettable voice and timeless talent, make Smokey Robinson a Rock 'N Roll Legend and Inspiration.

(sources: rockhall.com, theiceberg.com, rollingstone.com,VH1.com, rhythmandtheblues.org)

THE SUPREMES

(Featuring Diana Ross)

Diana Ross, Mary Wilson, and Florence Ballard, met in the 1950s, in Detroit's Brewster housing project. Originally known as the Primettes, they were a quartet, with Barbara Martin as fourth member.

In 1960, they made their first single for Lupine Records. In 1961, they debuted for Motown, and were renamed The Supremes, and also became a trio when Barbara Martin left after their first single. The Supremes' first Motown recordings were girl-group oriented. In the beginning, Florence Ballard was thought to have the best voice, and sang lead. But, by the time they got their first Top 40 hit in 1963, with "When The Lovelight Starts Shining Through His Eyes", Diana Ross had taken over as lead singer.

It's been said that Diana Ross was not the most talented female singer at Motown, Martha Reeves and Gladys Knight were considered to have had superior talent. But what Diana did have was pop appeal, rockstar personality, and glamour. This pop appeal theory paid off in 1964, when, the Holland-Dozier-Holland songs "Where Did Our Love Go", "Baby Love", "Stop! In the Name of Love", "Come See About Me", and "Back in My Arms Again", all became number one hits for the Supremes. Holland-Dozier-Holland would write and produce all of the Supremes' hits through 1967.

However, behind the bliss of success there were problems. Martha Reeves, and other Motown stars, resented the exorbitant attention Berry Gordy lavished upon Diana Ross. The other Supremes also felt increasingly pushed to the background by Diana and Berry. Consequently, in 1967, Florence Ballard was replaced in the Supremes by Cindy Birdsong, of Patti LaBelle and the Bluebelles. Sadly, Florence Ballard become one of rock's greatest tragedies, ending up on welfare, and dying broke in 1976. Also, after Florence was dismissed, the group would be billed as Diana Ross & The Supremes.

In 1967, Diana Ross & The Supremes had a big year, incorporating some psychedelic influences into the hit single "Reflections". Holland-Dozier-Holland left Motown around this time, and the quality of the Supremes' records suffered. The Supremes were still superstars, but as a group, they were falling apart. Their final hits were "Love Child" and "Someday We'll Be Together".

In November 1969, Diana Ross announced her departure for a solo career, and in January 1970, she played her last dates with the Supremes in Las Vegas. Jean Terrell replaced Diana in the Supremes, and the group continued through 1977, with some more changes, although Mary Wilson was always involved. Some of the singles were very good, particularly "Stoned Love", "Nathan Jones", and the Supremes and Four Tops collaboration on the re-make of "River Deep, Mountain High".

In 1970, following the release of "Reach Out And Touch (Somebody's Hand)", Diana Ross began a long series of successful solo releases with the hit "Ain't No Mountain High Enough". She continued to enjoy success with "I'm Still Waiting" which topped the UK charts in 1971. In April of that same year, Diana married businessman Robert Silberstein. Also in 1971, Berry Gordy's efforts to widen Diana's appeal led to a television special, and in 1972, she starred in the film, "Lady Sings The Blues". Diana received an Academy Award nomination for her dynamic and riveting portrayal of Billie Holiday's physical decline into drug addiction.

In 1973, Diana's single "Touch Me In The Morning" became a number one hit, and she released an album of duets with Marvin Gaye. In 1975 Diana starred in the film "Mahogany", and scored another number one hit with its theme song "Do You Know Where You're Going To" (Can we give a shout-out to Billy Dee Williams y'all!). Her fourth solo hit was "Love Hangover" in 1976, and she divorced Robert Silberstein that same year. In 1978, Diana starred in the film "The Whiz" with Michael Jackson (not to be confused with Billy Dee Williams y'all).

In 1980, Diana went disco with her album Diana, produced by Nile Rodgers and Bernard Edwards of Chic. She scored a major hit with "Upside Down", which stayed at the top of the charts for a month, and reached number two in the UK. She further scored hits with the singles "I'm Coming Out", "It's My Turn", and "My Old Piano". The following year a duet with Lionel Richie produced the title track to the movie "Endless Love", which spent more than two months at the top of the charts. Also in the 1980s, Diana became a closely watched media personality, gaining publicity for her relationship with the notorious fire breathing, and blood spitting heavy metal rockstar, Gene Simmons of Kiss.

In 1981, Diana Ross left Motown Records, and signed with RCA Records nationally, and Capitol Records internationally. She formed her own production company and had hits with "Why Do Fools Fall In Love", "Muscles" and 1984's "Missing You", a tribute to the late Marvin Gaye. In Britain she achieved a number one hit in 1986 with "Chain Reaction", written and produced by the Bee Gees. Also in 1986, Diana married Norwegian shipping magnate Arne Naess.

Diana continued to be very successful in the UK, scoring hits with "When You Tell Me That You Love Me" and "One Shining Moment". In 1994, she starred in the television movie "Out Of Darkness", playing a schizophrenic, and in 1999, Diana announced the end of her marriage to Arne Naess.

Collectively, The Supremes were the most successful African American musical group of the 1960s, and at one point had five number one singles in a row. The Supremes were the also most successful at infiltrating the radios and televisions of White America, an extraordinary achievement considering the tense social climate of the 1960s. In 2000, there was a Supremes reunion tour, featuring Diana Ross as the only original member. Unfortunately, the tour was cancelled due to poor ticket sales. However, the legacy of The Supremes lives on in a treasure of recordings and the beautiful memories of a time when three wonderful women ruled Rock 'N Roll.

(sources: the-supremes.com, rollingstone.com, theiceberg.com, VH1.com)

THE TEMPTATIONS

The Temptations formed in Detroit in 1961 as a merger of two local vocal groups, the Primes and the Distants. Baritone Otis Williams, bass vocalist Melvin Franklin, and Elbridge Bryant, sang together in the Distants, who recorded the single "Come On" for Detroit's Northern label in 1959. The Primes, a trio with tenor Eddie Kendricks, Paul Williams, and Kell Osborne, relocated to Detroit from Alabama, and quickly found local success. The Primes' manager also put together a girl group counterpart called the Primettes. Later, the Primettes' Diana Ross, Mary Wilson and Florence Ballard, would form the Supremes.

In 1961, the Primes disbanded, and Otis Williams, impressed by Eddie Kendricks' vocal prowess and Paul Williams' choreography skills, recruited both for his own group. Soon, Otis Williams, Melvin Franklin, Eddie Kendricks, Paul Williams, and Elbridge Bryant, joined together as the Elgins. After a name change to "The Temptations", they signed to the Motown Records' subsidiary Miracle, where they released a handful of singles over the next few months. Their 1962 single "Dream Come True", achieved commercial success, however, in 1963, Elbridge Bryant left the group after physically attacking Paul Williams.

In 1964, they recruited tenor David Ruffin to replace Bryant, and entered the studio with writer/producer Smokey Robinson to record the pop hit "The Way You Do the Things You Do". This single was the first in a series of 37 career Top Ten hits for the Temptations. In

1965, they recorded "My Girl", a number one hit, and Top 20 hits "It's Growing", "Since I Lost My Baby", "Don't Look Back", and "My Baby". In 1966, the Temptations recorded the hit, "Get Ready". After spotlighting Eddie Kendricks on the smash hit "Ain't Too Proud to Beg", the group allowed David Ruffin to sing lead on a string of hits including "Beauty's Only Skin Deep" and "(I Know) I'm Losing You".

Around 1967, their sound became rougher and more powerful, as exemplified on the 1968 hit "I Wish It Would Rain". That same year, the Temptations fired David Ruffin when he failed to appear at a live performance. David Ruffin was replaced by ex-Contour Dennis Edwards, and the group's success continued. In the late 1960s, the Temptations' music would reflect the times, and became very political with songs like "Cloud Nine" about drugs, "Run Away Child, Running Wild", "Psychedelic Shack", and "Ball of Confusion (That's What the World Is Today)".

In 1971, after the success of "Just My Imagination (Running Away with Me)", Eddie Kendricks left the Temptations for a solo career. Soon, Paul Williams, long plagued by alcoholism, also left the group. Tragically, in 1973, Paul Williams died from a self-inflected gunshot wound at the age of 34. The remaining Temptations recruited tenors Damon Harris and Richard Street, and after their 1971 hit "Superstar (Remember How You Got Where You Are)", they returned in 1972 with the number one single "Papa Was a Rolling Stone".

In 1973, the Temptations hit the charts again with "Masterpiece", "Let Your Hair Down", and "The Plastic Man". But, their success as a pop act gradually declined as the 1970s wore on. Damon Harris left the Temptations in 1975, and was replaced by tenor Glenn Leonard. In 1976, the group recorded their final album for Motown, "The Temptations Do the Temptations".

Louis Price took over for Dennis Edwards, and the Temptations signed to Atlantic Records in an attempt to reach the disco market with the albums "Bare Back" and "Hear to Tempt You". Dennis Edwards returned to the Temptations, resulting in Louis Price's exit, and the

Temptations re-signed with Motown, scoring the 1980 hit "Power".

In 1982, David Ruffin and Eddie Kendricks returned for the album "Reunion", which also included all five of the current Temptations. A tour followed, but personal differences, arguing, and problems with Motown, caused David and Eddie to exit again. In the late 1980s, Eddie Kendricks and Dennis Edwards performed as members of the "Tribute to the Temptations" package tour.

In 1988, Otis Williams published his autobiography, and by 1990, Otis was the only Temptation left from the original line-up. The following years were marked by tragedy. In 1991, David Ruffin died at age 50, after overdosing on cocaine. In October of 1992, Eddie Kendricks died at age 52 of lung cancer. Lastly, in February of 1995, Melvin Franklin died at age 52, after suffering a brain seizure.

In 1998, the Temptations returned with the album "Phoenix Rising". That same year, their story was told in an NBC miniseries, and the album "Earresistible" followed in the spring of 2000.

Thanks to their fine-tuned choreography, and even finer harmonies, the Temptations became the definitive male vocal group of the 1960s, and weathered six decades of changes in personnel and music stylings with grace and dignity. For their amazing career and unforgettable songs, The Temptations will forever be remembered as Rock 'N Roll Legends.

(sources: BarnesandNoble.com, rollingstone.com, theiceberg.com, VH1.com)

OTIS REDDING

(Born: September 19, 1941, Dawson, Georgia)

Born in Dawson, Georgia, Otis Redding's father was a Baptist Minister. At the age of five, his family moved to Macon, Georgia and at an early age young Otis began his career as a singer and musician in the choir of the Vineville Baptist Church. Otis attended Ballad Hudson High School and participated in the school band. However, to help his family financially, Otis dropped out of high school and went on to work with Little Richard's former band, the Upsetters. Otis began to compete in local talent shows for the five-dollar prize, but, after winning 15 times in a row, he was no longer allowed to enter the contests.

In 1959, Otis sang at the Grand Duke Club, and that same year he met his future wife Zelma Atwood. Otis joined Johnny Jenkins and the Pinetoppers in 1960, and would sing at the Teenage Party talent shows on Saturday mornings at the Roxy Theater, and later at the Douglas Theatre in Macon.

In 1962, Johnny Jenkins and the Pinetoppers drove to Memphis, Tennessee, for a recording session at Stax Records. Stax co-owner Jim Stewart, allowed Otis to cut a couple of songs with the studio time that had been booked, and the result was the single "These Arms of Mine", released in 1962. This was the first of many hit singles including "I've Been Loving You Too Long", "Respect", and "Try A Little Tenderness". In 1963, Otis was invited to perform at the Apollo Theatre for a live recording and showed his dance moves with "Shake" and

"Satisfaction". When Otis was done, the sold-out audience shouted and screamed, until Otis came back for an encore.

Otis Redding was a great businessman, and formed his own label, Jotis records, in 1965. In addition to his many business interests in music, Otis invested in real estate, stocks, bonds and a private plane. Otis knew how to earn and invest his money. He was able to purchase a 300-acre farm in Round Oak, Georgia. The farm had a two-story brick home, livestock, and a three and a half acre lake.

Otis Redding toured triumphantly throughout the United States, Canada, Europe, and the Caribbean. His concerts were among the biggest box office successes of the time. The National Academy of Recording Arts & Sciences nominated Otis in three categories for recordings he made during 1967. Remarkably, all songs written and arranged by Otis Redding himself led to his commercial success. Three of his songs alone accounted for over three and one half million record sales. Otis Redding was the president of his own publishing firm, and directly responsible for the company's leadership. To date, the company has copyrighted and published over 200 commercially successful songs, many having sold in excess of one million copies each.

The idea that music could bring people together was Otis' personal philosophy and reflected in his entire life. Otis had a White manager and a racially mixed band. Otis took care of business, he got paid and paid well without the usual rock 'n roll horror stories of being ripped off by promoters, agents, managers, or record companies.

Tragically, Otis Redding died when his own private plane crashed in 1967. Shortly afterwards, he scored the biggest hit of his career "(Sittin' On) The Dock Of The Bay". It was unlike anything he had ever written, and was reportedly influenced by the Beatles' "Sgt. Pepper's Lonely Hearts Club Band" album. Its been said that Otis played The Beatles' album constantly during a week he had spent on a houseboat in Sausalito, California, while performing at San Francisco's Fillmore West Theater, in the summer of 1967.

In 1970, Warner Bros. released an album of live recordings from the Monterey International Pop Festival of June 1967, featuring Otis Redding on one side and Jimi Hendrix on the other. In 1987, Atlantic Records released "The Otis Redding Story", a two volume record set featuring "I've Been Loving You Too Long", "Respect", "Pain in my Heart", "Satisfaction" and "The Dock Of The Bay". In 1995, Atlantic Records released "The Best of Otis Redding" which was a two record set including many of his most famous songs. "The Dock of the Bay" posthumously went on to become Otis Redding's biggest hit world-wide, and assured that Otis Redding will forever be remembered as a Rock 'N Roll Legend.

(sources: rollingstone.com, theiceberg.com, otisredding.com, VH1.com, rhythmandtheblues.org)

JACKIE WILSON

(born: June 9, 1934, Detroit, Michigan)

Jackie Wilson was born in Detroit, Michigan, and attended Highland Park High School, where he sang with Levi Stubbs, later of the Four Tops, in local clubs.

In 1953, Billy Ward, of Billy Ward and The Dominoes, saw 18-year old Jackie Wilson, at Detroit's Fox Theater. Billy was looking to replace his recently departed lead singer, and Billy really appreciated Jackie's vocal range and showmanship.

In 1957, Jackie left The Dominoes, went solo, and signed with Brunswick Records. His career gained momentum when he began performing songs co-written by Berry Gordy. These included "Reet Petite", "To Be Loved" and "Lonely Teardrops".

However, Brunswick Records was never able to settle on a particular musical style for Jackie. Jackie favored pop, where he could use his vocal range better, but Jackie's Brunswick recordings were frequently backed by an abundance of brass and strings.

It's been said that Jackie Wilson's best music emerged from his late '50s and early '60s era recordings. In 1961, while staying in a New York City hotel, Jackie Wilson was shot and seriously wounded by one of the women with whom he was involved. As a result of his injuries he lost a kidney and had to carry the bullet in his body for the rest of his life.

In 1966 and 1967, Jackie recorded the timeless soul classics "Whispers" and "Higher and Higher". Tragically, in September of

1975, while touring with the Dick Clark revue, Jackie suffered a heart attack onstage at New Jersey's Latin Casino. He struck his head as he fell, and the resulting brain damage left him comatosed. Though some reports say he had moments of clarity, Jackie Wilson had left the stage forever.

Jackie remained hospitalized until his death in January 1984. Some claim he was not in a coma, but totally paralyzed and unable to react to any stimuli. Sadly, The Great Jackie Wilson died on January 21, 1984, in Mount Holly, New Jersey, at Burlington County Memorial Hospital. The official cause of death was listed as pneumonia.

Tragically, Jackie Wilson further suffered the unforgivable and remarkably erroneous indignity of being buried in an unmarked grave in Detroit. This sad state of affairs was later corrected in 1987, and he was inducted into the Rock & Roll Hall of Fame that same year. Rightly, Jackie Wilson will always be remembered as an amazing singer, performer and Star-Bright Rock 'N Roll Hero!

(sources: thejackiewilsonstory.org, rollingstone.com, theiceberg.com, VH1.com)

SAM COOKE

(Born: January 22, 1931, Clarksdale, Mississippi)

Born in Clarksdale, Mississippi, Sam Cooke grew up in Chicago, one of eight sons of a Baptist minister. Having learned and sharpened his singing skills in the church, Sam was a top gospel artist by 1951, and as a teenager had become lead vocalist of the Soul Stirrers, with whom he toured and recorded for nearly six years.

In 1956, Sam Cooke recorded the single "Lovable" as Dale Cooke, but his record label dropped him for leaving the Soul Stirrers. However, it didn't take long, and soon after, Sam recorded the number one hit single "You Send Me" the following year, and it sold 1.7 million copies, making Sam Cooke a bonified mega star. In the next two years he had hits with "Only Sixteen" and "Everybody Likes to Cha Cha" in 1959.

In 1960, Sam Cooke signed to RCA Records and began writing blues and gospel influenced songs. Sam scored hits with "Chain Gang" and "Wonderful World" in 1960, "Sad Mood" in 1961, "Twistin' the Night Away" and "Bring It On Home to Me" in 1962, and "Another Saturday Night" in 1963. In addition to his songwriting and producing, Sam Cooke was a groundbreaking music entrepreneur. He owned his own record label, music publishing company, and management firm.

Tragically, Sam Cooke was shot to death in December of 1964. The manager of the Hacienda motel in Los Angeles, claimed she killed Sam after he attacked a young woman, and his shooting was ruled justifiable homicide by the Los Angeles coroner. In 1965, just two months after his death, Sam Cooke had another hit with the single

"Shake". Recording artist worldwide have covered Sam Cooke's songs; his hit single "Shake" was re-recorded by Otis Redding. Also in 1965, Sam Cooke's posthumous release "A Change Is Gonna Come" hit number 31 on the charts.

In 1986, Sam Cooke was one of the first inductees into the Rock and Roll Hall of Fame. Sam Cooke was a great songwriter, producer and performer who successfully merged gospel and secular music. His clear, strong vocals were widely imitated, and his suave style and sophisticated image set the standard for years to come, making Sam Cooke a Rock 'N Roll Legend.

(sources: theiceberg.com, rollingstone.com, VH1.com, rhythmandtheblues.org)

JAMES BROWN

(Born: May 3, 1933, Barnwell, South Carolina)

He was born James Joe Brown, Jr. in Barnwell, South Carolina. His father was Joe Garner Brown, and his mother was Susie Behlings Brown. Astoundingly, James Brown was a stillborn baby delivered by his aunts. When his aunts saw that baby James wasn't breathing, his aunt Minnie blew air into his lungs until James finally started crying.

James Brown's parents were very poor. His father made his living selling tree tar to a turpentine company, and they lived in a shack without plumbing or electricity, in the woods. James Brown's parents split up when he was four years old, and young James stayed with his father.

James Brown's father, Joe, was a hard working man, and did his best to raise James. Joe would work on farms and in gas stations when there was no turpentine work. Joe Brown eventually got James' aunt Minnie to stay with them and help out. The three of them decided to move across the Savannah River to Augusta, Georgia, so Joe could find better work, and they moved in with his aunt Honey. Joe soon left and never lived with James again, but stayed in close contact.

James Brown's aunt Honey ran a brothel and sold moonshine to the nearby military base. Young James would lead servicemen to the house, shine shoes, and dance on the street for change. Most of the money he made, he gave to Honey, and it was around this time that James became interested in music. He learned to play the harmonica, piano, and drums from people he met, and would practice every chance he got.

The brothel was eventually closed down, and Aunt Minnie and James moved into a cottage. James later learned to play the piano with both hands, and started sweeping floors of the Trinity Baptist Church so he could practice on their piano when no one was there. James played all types of music, and at age eleven, he entered an amateur night contest at the Lenox Theater and won first prize singing "So Long".

Along with music, James was interested in boxing, baseball, and football. Notably, James started getting into trouble around the age of fifteen, when he began stealing and joined a gang. He was caught stealing a car battery by the police, but his stealing didn't stop there. When James and some friends broke into some cars one night, the police caught James and put him in jail. James Brown turned sixteen in jail before he was brought to trial, and charged with four counts of breaking and entering, and larceny. James was found guilty and sentenced to eight to sixteen years in prison.

While in prison, James Brown returned to his music. James tried to make the best of his time in prison. He became close to the warden who treated him like a son, and James started a gospel quartet that included Johnny Terry who became a member of the Famous Flames. The prison had a piano in the gym, and James was eventually allowed to play it.

It was in prison that James Brown first heard about Bobby Byrd, and they eventually met through the prison fence. James wrote a letter to the Parole Board asking for early release. Someone from the Parole Board came to visit him and James said that he wanted to sing gospel if he was released. James made a good impression, and was released the next day, just three years and one day after his conviction. There were, of course, some conditions. James could not return to Augusta where his family lived, and he had to find work and a place to live.

The newly free James Brown ended up in Toccoa, Georgia, working at a car dealership and lived with Bobby Byrd's family. This was the beginning of a long relationship between James and Bobby, and in 1952, James Brown and Bobby Byrd started a quartet called the Gospel Starlighters. The group's southern gospel style was inspired by the great gospel groups of that era, and the Starlighters later changed their name to the Flames.

In November 1955, while based in Macon, Georgia, the Flames cut a demo record of the song "Please, Please, Please". Record producer Ralph Bass heard the demo and was so impressed with James Brown's vocals and the group's harmonies, that he signed them to King Records. A session was held in Ohio and the single was released two months later.

In 1956, James Brown and the Flames scored a hit with "Please, Please, Please", which reached number five on the Billboard's R&B chart. James had made it a hit by performing it across the country. There was no promotion by the record company, so when they got to New York, they signed with Universal booking which provided more gigs. Universal later asked them to change the name of the group to James Brown and the Famous Flames, and they continued to make records, but it would be nearly three years before they had another hit on the charts.

In 1957, Little Richard retired from music to study theology, and James Brown was called to fill his bookings. James performed with the Upsetters and the Dominions, recruited a new band from members of the Dominions, and recorded "Try Me". In late 1958, early 1959, James Brown scored another hit with "Try Me", giving his group its first number one recording, and enabling James Brown to hire a professional backup band. Over time, James Brown developed the band into the hottest group around. James' stunning stage show and the band's flawless timing, made every show an event.

In 1962, James Brown felt that the hysteria he was generating in concert could be captured on an album. But, King Records didn't think the album would sell, so James Brown put up his own money and recorded a performance at the Apollo Theater. Released in 1964, "Live at The Apollo" went to number two on the album charts. Radio stations played it with a frequency formerly reserved for singles, and the audiencces at James Brown's concerts exploded with excitement to see him perform. Reflective of his newfound popularity, James Brown would record with the Famous Flames for the last time in June of 1964 before embarking upon his solo career.

Now on his own, in 1965, James Brown scored his first top ten pop single with "Papa's Got A Brand New Bag". The songs beat was accented on the first and third beats instead of the traditional second and fourth beats. The difference was in the rhythm, it was on "the one". James used an off beat bass line, while the horns and guitars played contrasting rhythms, creating a new sound that changed R&B.

The 1960s were a turbulent time for Black people in America. Segregation, poverty, drugs, and the unequal drafting of the poor and minorities into the Vietnam War, were some of the problems that Black people faced. The night after Dr. Martin Luther King's assassination, James Brown was scheduled to play the Boston Garden. James flew to Boston to perform, but was met by a Black councilman and was told that the mayor wanted to cancel the concert. James convinced the mayor to change his mind when he suggested that the concert be televised. James felt that if people stayed home to watch his concert, there would be no rioting. James arranged permission to televise the concert and the Mayor guaranteed the box office receipts. Consequently, there was no rioting in Boston.

In 1968, James Brown went to Vietnam to play for the US Troops, and returned to a hotbed of controversy. Some in the Black community felt that going to Vietnam showed that James Brown supported the government's position on the war. Some even criticized James, and called him an "Uncle Tom". James' song "America Is My Home", was also fuel for the criticism.

In response, James Brown recorded a song in support of the Black Power movement. James wrote "Say It Loud (I'm Black And I'm Proud)". The song became a catalyst for the movement, and a number one hit single. The song was an anthem that showed Black pride and defiance. But it had cost James, he had offended the White establishment, and soon after his problems with the FBI and IRS began (…coincidence?).

It's a well-known fact, that James Brown's horn section was one of the tightest of all time. However, James was very controlling, and this led to an eventual fallout with his band. In 1970, the band was in Columbus, Georgia, for a concert, and the members were upset with James, and refused to play. So, James called his agent to find The Pacemakers, a band that toured with Hank Ballard and Marva Whitney. The Pacemakers were a teenage band that included the brothers "Bootsy" and "Catfish" Collins on bass & guitar. The Pacemakers were called, and flown to Columbus to perform behind James that night. James fired his band, and played the concert with the new band along with Bobby Byrd and "Jabo" Starks.

James Brown's new players were first named the "New Breed Band", but eventually became "The JB's". Bootsy Collins' rhythmic bass style gave the band a new dynamic and brought Bootsy into the spotlight. Bootsy based his style on the percussive slap and pluck bass playing of Sly and The Family Stone's bassist, Larry Graham. James began making new arrangements of his old hits for The JB's, turning songs like "Give It Up, Turn It Loose" into "Get Up I Feel Like Being A Sex Machine". The JB's took James Brown to a new level of music, and the public loved them. Songs like "Licking Stick" and "Cold Sweat" were crowd favorites.

James Brown was no stranger to controversy, and had a number of difficulties, including his early prison stay for theft, financial and tax problems, and a drug problem that landed him in prison. However, things got worse when in 1988, after James Brown's wife brought assault and battery charges against him, and after a year of going through legal and personal troubles, James Brown (its been said) threatened some people in one of his buildings with a gun. What followed was the legendary high-speed interstate car chase between the police and an allegedly inebriated James Brown. For this, James went back to prison, but was paroled in two years (Free James Brown!).

James Brown's status as "The Godfather of Soul" has been embraced by a new generation of fans that have become familiar with his music through its frequent use as samples on rap records, and in popular films and culture. A highly respected and charter member of the Rock and Roll Hall of Fame, in 1992, James Brown received a special Lifetime Achievement Grammy Award for his many years of standard setting excellence in music.

Today James Brown's music is finally recognized as some of the most important in all of Rock 'N Roll. James Brown's rise from juvenile delinquent to Soul Brother #1, is among the great American success stories. He is 'The Godfather of Soul', and over a 50-year career, James Brown earned 17 number one hit singles, and 98 entries on the top 40 R&B singles charts, a record unsurpassed by any other artist, making James Brown a Rock 'N Roll Hero, Legend, and Icon.

(sources: topblacks.com, rollingstone.com, soul-patrol.com, theiceberg.com, VH1.com)

RICHIE HAVENS

(Born: January 21, 1941, Brooklyn, New York)

Born in Brooklyn, New York, Richard Havens was the eldest of nine children who grew up in the Bedford-Stuyvesant community. His father was a self-taught piano player who worked with a number of bands around the city. When Richie was young, he organized a series of street corner doo-wop groups and at age 16, he sang with The Mc-Crea Gospel Singers. Richie sang doo-wop until the age of 20, at which point he went to enjoy the beatnik lifestyle of Greenwich Village. Richie saw Greenwich Village as a place where he could more openly express himself, and went there to perform poetry in the late 1950s.

Richie began performing on guitar in the early '60s, and gained a reputation as a solo performer. He recorded two albums worth of demos in 1965 and 1966, and landed his first deal with Verve Records, which released his album "Mixed Bag" in 1967. Richie's debut album featured the single "Handsome Johnny", co-written by Richie and Lou Gossett Jr., the song "Follow", later heard on the soundtrack to the 1978 film "Coming Home", and Bob Dylan's "Just Like A Woman".

In 1968, the record "Something Else Again" became Richie's first album to hit the charts, and its popularity pulled his previous release, "Mixed Bag", onto the charts as well. That same year, Douglas International added instrumental tracks to Richie's old demos and released two albums worth of material. By the late 1960s, Richie Havens was in high demand at colleges across the country, and on the international folk and pop concert circuit. Richie played the Newport Folk Festival in 1966, the Monterey Jazz Festival in 1967, the Miami Pop Festival in 1968, and Woodstock in 1969.

Richie Havens' Woodstock performance was a major turning point in his career. As the festival's opening act, Richie performed in front of the multitudes of people for nearly three hours. Remarkably, when he was cheered back for another encore, he improvised a song based on the old Negro Spiritual "Motherless Child" that became his hit song "Freedom".

In 1970, Richie Havens signed with Stormy Forest/MGM Records, who released his "Stonehenge" album. Later that same year came the album "Alarm Clock", which yielded the top 20 single "Here Comes The Sun", written by George Harrison of The Beatles. More albums followed, including "The Great Blind Degree" in 1971, "Richie Havens On Stage" in 1972, "Portfolio" in 1973, and "Mixed Bag II" in 1974.

Further expanding his artistic expression, Richie Havens began acting during the 1970s. In 1972, Richie was featured in the original stage presentation of The Who's rock opera "Tommy". In 1974, he was the lead in the film "Catch My Soul", and In 1977, Richie co-starred with Richard Pryor in the film "Greased Lightning".

During the 1970's and 1980's, Richie toured constantly, and recorded the albums "The End Of The Beginning", "Mirage", "Connections", "Common Ground", "Simple Things" and "Now". In the 1990s, Richie continued his dauntless touring pace. In 1993, Richie Havens performed at the Bill Clinton's Presidential Inauguration, and released "Resume: The Best Of Richie Havens on Rhino Records", a collection of his late '60s and early '70s recordings. This effort was followed by the album "Cuts To The Chase", also released on Rhino Records.

In 2002, Richie Havens recorded and released the album "Wishing Well" which included the singles "Paradise", and "On The Turning Away". Also that year, re-mastered CD versions of Richie's early albums, "Stonehenge", "Alarm Clock", "Portfolio", "The Great Blind Degree", "Richie Havens On Stage", and "Mixed Bag II", were released.

For over 40 years, Richie Havens has used his music to convey messages of brotherly love and freedom. An undaunted and prolific recording artist since he first emerged from the Greenwich Village folk scene in the early 1960s, Richie Havens has weathered the change of more that a few rock 'n roll seasons. His legendary longevity, and commitment to peace, make Richie Havens a Rock 'N Roll Hero and Folk Music Legend.

(sources: onlinetalent.com, rollingstone.com, richiehavens.com, VH1.com)

JIMI HENDRIX

(Born: November 27, 1942, Seattle, Washington)

James Marshal Hendrix was born in Seattle, Washington, in 1942. An unsettled home environment made Jimi spend much of his early years living in Canada with his grandmother, a full-blooded Cherokee Indian. When Jimi was 12 he got the instrument which shaped the rest of his life, an electric guitar. Sadly, Jimi's mother died when he was 15, and at 16, Jimi was thrown out of school for holding the hand of a White girl. But this just fueled his music, because by this time Jimi was taking his performing seriously, and passionately played rock 'n roll in bands until he joined the army at age 17.

Jimi Hendrix played in a band while in the service, but after 14 months as a paratrooper, Jimi suffered an injury and was discharged from the Army. The next four years he toured the US playing guitar for R&B bands, including Little Richard, Ike & Tina Turner, Wilson Pickett, and King Curtis. Eventually, Jimi ended up in Greenwich Village, New York, where he recorded with the Isley Brothers, and Curtis Knight.

In 1965, Jimi formed his own band, "Jimmy James and the Blue Flames". They played the Greenwich Village clubs where word of the young genius reached ex-Animals bassist Chas Chandler. Chas was so impressed after hearing Jimi play that he offered to be his manager, and take Jimi to England.

In 1966, England was ruled by The Beatles, The Who, Cream, and electric guitar legends Eric Clapton, Jimmy Page and Jeff Beck.

Now suddenly, there was this Black guy from America doing things with the guitar that seemed impossible. Jimi Hendrix quickly gained the respect of his peers and adoration of the masses. The Jimi Hendrix Experience was formed, and they toured Europe, breaking attendance records at every club they played.

Jimi signed a recording contract, and a series of singles followed, including "Hey Joe", "The Wind Cries Mary" and "Purple Haze". Jimi became a star in England, and his stunning performance at the Monterey Pop Festival, which he ended by holding his burning guitar above his head, instantly made him a celebrity in America. Jimi's albums sold millions of copies and his tours sold-out. 1967, was a very good year for Jimi, impressively, he had four singles and two albums on the British charts and two albums on the US charts.

Very quickly and semi-reluctantly, Jimi Hendrix became a rock idol, and the blind adoration of his audiences frustrated the serious musician in him. Jimi would smash his guitar to pieces because he felt he played badly, and the crowd would love it. Jimi's moods worsened within the loneliness of stardom, and he became sullen and unapproachable to many. In 1968 Jimi was jailed in Sweden for trashing a hotel room.

However moody, the records Jimi recorded during those years were amazing, "Are You Experienced?" and "Axis: Bold As Love" are still popular sellers to this day. Also in 1968, the album "Electric Ladyland", was released and produced the hit "All Along The Watchtower", written by Bob Dylan. In 1969, Jimi's band The Experience split up and Jimi joined up with bassist Billy Cox to play at Woodstock. At Woodstock, Jimi only played his now famous "Star Spangled Banner" and one other tune, before walking off the stage because he felt it wasn't coming together. Once again ironically it didn't matter, because the only thing the audience cared about was that Jimi Hendrix was there. It didn't matter how well he played, just that he played, a fact that continued to frustrate Jimi to no end.

In 1970, Jimi formed "Band Of Gypsies" with Buddy Miles on

drums and Billy Cox on bass, and the short-lived group recorded one album, which became a major hit. Jimi returned to England in August of that same year, and played at the 3rd "Isle Of Wight" festival. Afterward, he embarked on a tour of Europe. Unfortunately, bassist Billy Cox had a nervous breakdown, and had to be flown home to the United States. Disappointed, and his frustrations intensifying, Jimi returned to London.

Upon his return to in London, Jimi reportedly went on a sex and drug binge, which resulted in an over-dose of sleeping pills in a woman's flat. An ambulance was called, but Jimi was seated upright in the back with no head support, and sometime during the twenty-five minute ride to St. Mary Abbot's Hospital, The Great Jimi Hendrix choked to death on his own vomit. He was pronounced Dead On Arrival (DOA). The pathologist reported a large amount of Seconol in Jimi's blood, but found no reason to assume that suicide was the cause of death.

Jimi Hendrix personified Rock 'N Roll Genius. Today, over thirty years after Jimi's tragic death, the Hendrix family owns an empire based on Jimi's music, worth over 150 million dollars. Jimi Hendrix remains the Icon of Rock Guitar, and hands down, the most celebrated guitarist of all-time!

(sources: hotshotdigital.com, rollingstone.com, theiceberg.com, VH1.com)

the

'70s

In the 1970s, African American Rock 'N Roll Artists had a positive impact on the Social-Economic progress of Blacks in American cities and urban communities.

The increased visibility of Black Rock musicians and their displays of wealth and income in magazines, on TV, and at grand concert extravaganzas, created a blueprint for affluent African American lifestyles in big cities and westernized culture.

MARVIN GAYE

(Born: April 2, 1939, Washington, DC)

Marvin Pentz Gay Jr. was born in Washington, DC, in 1939, and was named after his father, Marvin Gay Sr., a minister. The church influenced young Marvin's early years, and played a important role in his musical career, as his songwriting shifted back and forth between secular and religious topics. Eventually, young Marvin left his father's church choir and joined the Rainbows, a R&B vocal group.

In 1957, Marvin joined the Marquees, who recorded for Chess Records under the supervision of the legendary Bo Diddley. In 1960, Marvin moved to Detroit, went to work with Berry Gordy at Motown Records, and became a session drummer and vocalist. In 1961, Marvin married Berry Gordy's sister, Anna, and signed a solo recording contract with Motown Records as a jazz singer. Marvin also changed the spelling of his last name from Gay, to Gaye.

In 1962, Marvin crossed over to R&B, and released his first top ten R&B hit single "Stubborn Kind Of Fellow". Over the next three years, Marvin enjoyed a series of hits. He also continued his writing and session work at Motown, co-writing Martha And The Vandellas' hit "Dancing In The Street", and playing drums on Stevie Wonder's early recordings.

In 1965, Marvin began to record in a more sophisticated style with songs like "How Sweet It Is (To Be Loved By You)", and the number one R&B hits, "I'll Be Doggone" and "Ain't That Peculiar". With these efforts, Marvin achieved the status of Motown's best-selling male vocalist.

To capitalize on Marvin's "Ladies' Man" image, Motown teamed him up with their leading female vocalist, Mary Wells, for romantic duets. When Mary Wells left Motown in 1964, Marvin recorded with Kim Weston until 1967. In 1967, Marvin Gaye was teamed up with female vocalist Tammi Terrell, and the Marvin and Tammi partnership represented the high point of the soul duets. Marvin and Tammi's voices blended beautifully on a string of hit songs written specifically for the duo by the famed songwriting team Nick Ashford and Valerie Simpson.

In 1968, tragedy struck when Tammi Terrell developed a brain tumor and collapsed onstage in Marvin's arms. Interestingly, recordings continued to be released under the duo's name, although it could not have been Tammi singing on the records. Later in 1968, Marvin released the hit single "I Heard It Through The Grapevine", and it became Motown's biggest-selling record to date. Marvin followed this up with the number one hit "Too Busy Thinking 'Bout My Baby".

In 1970, Marvin Gaye's career came to a sudden halt, when Tammi Terrell died in March of 1970. Marvin was devastated by Tammi's death, and spent most of 1970 in seclusion and grief. In 1971, a now sullen and more introspective Marvin Gaye emerged with a set of recordings that Motown at first refused to release. That album was "What's Going On", Marvin Gaye's most successful solo album. Hit singles from this ground breaking album included, the number one hits "What's Going On", "Mercy Mercy Me" and "Inner City Blues". "What's Going On" reflected Marvin Gaye's concerns about poverty, discrimination, political corruption, and spirituality.

In 1972, Marvin composed the soundtrack to the 'Blaxploitation' thriller "Trouble Man". The title song gave Marvin Gaye another hit single. Curiously, Marvin Gaye began shifting his attention from political and spiritual topics to sex, with the hit single "Let's Get It On". The songs explicit sexuality marked a change in Marvin Gaye's career and life condition, Marvin began to use cocaine.

In 1973, Marvin collaborated with Diana Ross on an album of duets, and in 1975, Marvin's marriage to Anna Gordy ended. In 1977,

Marvin had a major hit with "Got To Give It Up", but drug and tax problems interrupted his career, and he flew to Hawaii in an attempt to salvage his failing second marriage. In 1979, Marvin devoted the year to the double album "Here, My Dear", which was a sad commentary on his relationship with his first wife Anna. Interestingly, Marvin had been ordered to give all royalties from that album to Anna as part of their divorce settlement.

In 1980, under increasing scrutiny from the IRS, Marvin Gaye moved to Europe where he began work on the album "In My Lifetime". But, in 1981, when it was released, Marvin accused Motown of re-mixing and editing the album and cover artwork without his consent. As a result, that next year Marvin Gaye left Motown for Columbia Records.

In 1982, Marvin had a smash hit with the single "Sexual Healing", from the album "Midnight Love". Marvin returned to the states, and went to live with his parents. Sadly, the level of his cocaine addiction made it impossible for him to work on his music, and he fell into a deep depression.

Reportedly, Marvin repeatedly announced he was going to commit suicide in the early weeks of 1984, and his drug altered moods brought him into violent conflict with his father. On April 1st, 1984, another in a line of drug induced violent disputes provoked Marvin Gay Sr. to shoot and kill his son.

Marvin Gaye's remarkable musical career, and inspiring songs remain a symbol of an era when greatness, talent, and awareness all came together in one artist, making Marvin Gaye a Rock 'N Roll Legend and Icon!

(sources: rhythmandtheblues.org, theiceberg.com, rollingstone.com, VH1.com)

STEVIE WONDER

(Born: May 13, 1950, Saginaw, Michigan)

Stevie Wonder was born Steveland Judkins, though he now prefers to be known as Steveland Morris after his mother's married name. Infant Stevie was placed in an incubator immediately after his birth, and was given too much oxygen, which caused him to suffer permanent blindness.

When little Stevie's family moved to Detroit, his mother was afraid to let seven-year-old Stevie out of the house. So, Stevie would stay inside and beat spoons on pots and pans to the rhythm of the songs on the radio. Despite little Stevie's blindness, he learned the piano at the age of seven, and the harmonica and drums by nine.

In 1954, Stevie joined a church gospel choir in Detroit. In 1961, Stevie was discovered by Ronnie White, of the Miracles, who arranged an audition at Motown Records. Berry Gordy signed Stevie to Motown, and renaming him 'Little Stevie Wonder'. In 1963, Stevie released the live recording "Fingertips" which established Stevie as a successful Motown artist. Berry Gordy and Motown marketed Stevie, calling him "The 12-year-old Genius", in an obvious attempt to link him with the popularity of "The Genius", Ray Charles.

In 1964, Stevie's career was placed on hold while his voice changed, and he continued recording in 1965, scoring a hit with "Uptight (Everything's Alright)".

Stevie Wonder was marketed like all the other Motown stars, and from 1965 to 1970, recorded material was chosen for him by Motown executives. However, Stevie co-wrote almost all of his Motown singles from 1967 on, and collaborated on songs by other Motown artists, co-writing Smokey Robinson and The Miracles' hit "The Tears Of A Clown", and writing and producing the Spinners' "It's A Shame".

Although Stevie played, wrote, and co-produced many of the songs on his albums, Motown still maintained tight control over his professional and personal life, and this frustrated young Stevie. In September of 1970, Stevie Wonder married fellow Motown artist Syreeta. In 1971, Stevie turned twenty-one, his contract with Motown expired, and rather than re-signing immediately as the label expected, Stevie opted out of his contract with Motown. The split from Motown was bitter. Stevie starting his own studio, and was able to explore his own musical direction. Stevie made records that combined elements of gospel, jazz, rock, Latin, and African rhythms. Stevie financed the recording of two albums of his own material, and played almost all the instruments himself. He then used these recordings to persuade Motown to offer him a more open contract, which gave him total artistic control over his music and the rights to the music publishing in his own company. Now a grown and married man, the adult Stevie Wonder made amends with Berry Gordy, and Motown distributed the albums "Music of My Mind" and "Where I'm Coming From".

In 1972, Stevie Wonder went on tour opening for the Rolling Stones. This widespread introduction to White audiences was significant to his success as an adult artist. Stevie also released the album "Talking Book" that same year. This album produced the hit singles "Superstition" and "You Are The Sunshine Of My Life". In 1973, Stevie enjoyed even more success with the album "Innervisions", which yielded the hit singles "Living For The City" and "Higher Ground". However, tragedy struck later that year, and Stevie was seriously injured in a car accident (official reports determined the Stevie was not driving at the time of the accident). Ever the consummate artist, Stevie Wonder used the inspiration from this traumatic experience to reaffirm him spiritually, emotionally, and artistically. As Stevie recovered from his injuries, he was inspired to create his most celebrated music to date.

In 1974, Stevie released the album "Fulfillingness' First Finale", and two years later in 1976, Stevie Wonder released the hit double album "Songs In The Key Of Life", inspired by his near death experience two years earlier. It included the hit singles "Sir Duke" and "Black Man", and this modern music masterpiece solidified Stevie Wonder's status as one of the most important songwriters and performance artists in contemporary music.

Stevie's next project was the soundtrack to the documentary "The Secret Life Of Plants". In 1980, Stevie Wonder released the highly successful "Hotter Than July", which included the Martin Luther King tribute song "Happy Birthday", and hit single "Masterblaster (Jamming)". In 1982, Stevie released the retrospective double album "Stevie Wonder's Original Musiquarium I", which included four new recordings alongside his favorite adult hits. In 1983, Stevie composed the soundtrack music for the film "The Woman In Red", which included his biggest-selling single "I Just Called To Say I Loved You". In 1985, Stevie released "In Square Circle" and "Characters" in 1987.

In the early 1980's, Stevie Wonder led a campaign to have Dr. Martin Luther King's birthday declared a national holiday, and helped to persuade then US. President Ronald Reagan to pass the needed legislation. Reflectively, the first Federal Holiday celebrating the birth of Dr. Martin Luther King Jr. was celebrated on January 15, 1986, with a concert headlined by Stevie Wonder himself.

Stevie Wonder has performed, written, and produced, with other artist, including work with ex-Beatle Paul McCartney, which produced the enormous hit, "Ebony And Ivory", and on the benefit records by USA for Africa and Dionne Warwick and Friends. In the 1990's, Stevie Wonder produced the soundtrack for Spike Lee's film "Jungle Fever", and released the album "Conversation Peace", which won two Grammys for the single "For Your Love". In 1996, Stevie Wonder was honored with a well-deserved Grammy Lifetime Achievement Award.

Stevie Wonder was one of the first inductees into the Rock and

Roll Hall of Fame. His long career has been remarkable for his musical genius, and his persistence in overcoming obstacles that would have stifled lesser persons. Further, Stevie's humanitarian and anti-apartheid work was acknowledged when he was invited to meet with South African President Nelson Mandela, who said, "Stevie Wonder is my son, and I speak to him with great affection." The amazing artist that is Stevie Wonder is a Rock 'N Roll Hero, Legend and Icon!

(sources: topblacks.com, rollingstone.com, theiceberg.com, VH1.com)

ROBERTA FLACK

(Born: February 10, 1937, Asheville, North Carolina)

Born in North Carolina to a musical family, Roberta Flack was inspired by her father, a church organist, to begin playing piano at a young age. Roberta went on to win a music scholarship to Howard University in Washington, D.C., and graduated from Howard with a BA in music.

Roberta Flack was discovered singing and playing jazz in a Washington D.C. nightclub by pianist Les McCann, who recommended her to Atlantic Records. At Atlantic, Roberta recorded two albums, "First Take" and "Chapter Two", achieving huge success with the single, "First Time Ever I Saw Your Face" three years later. In 1972, Roberta had a hit with "Where Is The Love", a duet with Donny Hathaway. "Killing Me Softly With His Song" was a hit in 1973, "The Closer I Get To You" in 1978, and "Back Together Again" with Donny Hathaway was released in 1980. Tragically, Roberta's longtime duet partner Donny Hathaway committed suicide in 1979, and Roberta was shattered.

In the 1980s, Roberta Flack enjoyed a successful partnership with singer Peabo Bryson that produced the 1983 hit single "Tonight I Celebrate My Love". Most deservedly, in the 1990s, Roberta Flack was re-introduced to a new generation of appreciative and adoring fans when her 1973 smash hit "Killing Me Softly With His Song" was re-recorded by hot pop sensations Lauryn Hill and the Fugees.

Roberta Flack is an inspiration to singers and musicians worldwide, and her smooth voice and endearing songs make her a Rock 'N Roll Hero to millions.

(sources: rollingstone.com, theiceberg.com, VH1.com)

THE JACKSON 5

(Featuring Michael Jackson)

T he Jackson 5 were formed in Gary, Indiana, and comprised of the young children of Joseph and Katherine Jackson. Jackie, Tito, Jermaine, Marlon and Michael Jackson rehearsed endlessly under the supervision of their father Joseph, winning many talent shows and performing around town.

In 1968, The Jackson 5 were brought to the attention of Berry Gordy and Motown. Berry Gordy promised the Jackson 5 three number one records, and "ABC", "I Want You Back", and "The Love You Save" all reached number one on the pop and R&B singles charts.

The Jackson 5 achieved fame in America and around the world, Initially, Joseph included young Michael in the lineup as just a novelty, but it became immediately obvious that his young son had great performing abilities. Young Michael Jackson possessed great control and maturity in his voice, and even more amazingly, Michael was a crowd-charming charismatic entertainer who possessed an innate genius that gifted him with the skills of a seasoned performer. Reflectively, Joseph Jackson was approached by Motown to have Michael to do solo recordings. In 1971, Michael Jackson's first single, "I'll Be There" reached number 4 on the singles charts. In addition to his work with The Jackson 5, Michael recorded the hit singles "Rockin' Robin" and "Ben".

A major part of the Jackson 5's success was due to the young ages of the brothers. However, as they grew older, Motown did not attempt to change the group's image or the lighthearted songs they were recording. The Jackson's wanted more creative control over their music, but Motown had a notoriously tight system in place. Consequently, The Jackson 5 left Motown, and Joseph signed the brothers with Epic Records so his sons would have the freedom to grow and express themselves musically. But singer/bassist Jermaine Jackson, who was married to Berry Gordy's daughter Hazel, chose to remain with his new family, and Motown.

Begrudgingly, Motown owned and kept the name "Jackson 5", and would not release it, so the group was forced to change their group name to "The Jacksons" under the Epic label, and add youngest brother Randy Jackson to once again give them five members.

In 1978, Michael starred opposite Diana Ross in the movie "The Wiz", an African American remake of The Wizard of Oz. The project introduced Michael Jackson to legendary producer Quincy Jones, who arranged and produced the film's music. In 1979, Michael and Quincy collaborated on Michael's next solo album "Off the Wall", which transformed Michael Jackson the child star, into Michael Jackson the adult superstar. The album included the hit singles "Don't Stop 'Til You Get Enough" and "Rock With You" and sold over ten million copies.

In 1982, Michael and Quincy collaborated on the album "Thriller", which sold over 40 million copies, more than any other album in history, before or since. "Thriller" won eight Grammy awards and charted six top ten singles, including a duet with Paul McCartney "The Girl Is Mine", the title track "Thriller", "Billie Jean", and "Beat It". Thriller's momentum was sustained with the help of the new promotion medium of music videos, which were gaining popularity thanks to the new 24-hour music video network, MTV.

In 1984, The Jacksons hit a professional high, when they re-teamed with brother Michael for the Victory tour. Michael's next albums, Bad in 1987 and Dangerous in 1991, both topped the charts and sold millions of copies. Mysteriously, over time, Michael Jackson was visually becoming Caucasian-looking, reportedly due to plastic surgery and make-up. In addition, stories of Michael's odd habits like the fact that he kept a coffin, white mannequins, and a shrine to Elizabeth Taylor in his home, began to surface. Most notably in the 1990s, a media scandal surfaced and grew into a worldwide frenzy, painting Michael as having an inappropriate relationship with a young boy.

In 1993, Michael Jackson consented to an interview with Oprah Winfrey, and a huge prime-time audience tuned in to watch him discuss his noticeably peculiar life condition. In the interview with Oprah, Michael attributed his bleached appearance to skin pigmentation deficiency and plastic surgery procedures. He also defended his romantic affiliations by naming the well-known actress Brooke Shields as a girlfriend, who coincidentally announced her engagement to tennis superstar Andre Agassi just days later. The interview succeeded in making Michael seem semi-normal for an entertainer of such mega proportion.

In 1994, Michael Jackson married Elvis Presley's daughter, Lisa Marie Presley, in a secret ceremony in the Dominican Republic. In 1995, Michael released a double album of his biggest hits and new songs entitled "HIStory", and teamed up for a duet with sister Janet Jackson, by then a superstar in her own right, on the hit single "Scream". The single "Scream" flaunted a fantastically futuristic 8 million dollar music video (saying "I've got 8 million to blow on a video and you don't… so shut-up!"), and earned them both a Grammy Award.

Also in 1995, the newlywed Michael and Lisa Marie, sat down for a prime-time interview with Diane Sawyer of ABC News, in which the couple insisted that their marriage was real. However, about 18 months later, they split-up. In 1996, Michael announced that a female friend was carrying his child, and Michael Jackson and Deborah Rowe were married in Australia. Three months later, Debbie gave birth to Prince Michael Jackson Jr., and in 1998, Michael's Daughter Paris Michael Katherine was born. However, in 1999, the couple semi-predictably announced their mutual decision to divorce, with Michael keeping the children.

In 2001, Michael released the album "Invincible", and produced a tribute concert for himself at Madison Square Garden. A host of celebrities turned out to honor Michael and celebrate his 30 years as a solo entertainer. Most notably, Michael's brothers turned out to perform a spectacular medley of their greatest hits as a group. But semi-surprisingly, and mostly disappointingly, again in 2003, another worldwide frenzy erupted when Michael was accused of having another inappropriate relationship with another young boy (Damn!).

Since leaving Motown, the Jackson 5 have reunited on stage for various occasions, most notably, the Motown 25 TV special in 1983, the Victory tour in 1984, and Michael's 30th Anniversary Celebration in 2001. As a family, the Jacksons have amazed, entertained, and endeared themselves into the collective consciousness and hearts of the world. All tell-all, kiddy, and tiddy, controversy aside, for their 40 plus years of dedication to musical and performing excellence, the Jackson 5, and the Jackson family, are unquestionably Rock 'N Roll Legends and Icons.

(sources: theiceberg.com, angelfire.com, topblacks.com, rollingstone.com, VH1.com)

EARTH WIND AND FIRE

Maurice White founded Earth Wind and Fire in 1971. Originally on Warner Bros. Records, in 1972, record industry legend Clive Davis signed the band to Columbia Records. In 1973, after their first gold album, Earth Wind and Fire produced six consecutive Double Platinum albums. In 1975, Earth Wind & Fire were the first Black act to top the pop single and album charts simultaneously, with the single "Shining Star" and the album "That's The Way Of The World". Also, they were the first Black act to receive Columbia Records Crystal Globe Award, signifying five million albums sold outside of the US.

Reflectively, Earth Wind & Fire are the top selling band in Columbia Records History, the first Black act to tour with a completely self-contained stage production, and headline an arena world tour without an opening act. They were also the first Black act to bring a full production to South America, and in 1980, were the first Black act to receive Madison Square Garden's Gold Ticket Award for 100,000 tickets sold.

However, before all of the fame and fortune, there was only a vision, and a dynamic visionary. Memphis-born and Chicago-raised Maurice White was the drummer of the renowned jazz pianist Ramsey Lewis and session drummer for Chess Records. Maurice wanted to form a band that found inspiration in all styles of music. So, he moved to Los Angeles, and convinced his younger brother Verdine to join him. Verdine White was a classically trained bassist who had never been outside of Chicago, so this was a considerable leap of faith, even for a brother.

Their first group was called "The Salty Peppers", but Maurice later renamed the band "Earth, Wind & Fire". They added a powerful young singer-percussionist from Denver named Philip Bailey and a drummer from Los Angeles named Ralph Johnson. Maurice's tenor and Philip's falsetto personified the band's vocal identity, and their styles fit together perfectly.

In the studio, Maurice composed elaborate vocal arrangements over wonderfully complex music. Earth, Wind & Fire produced the soundtrack to the pioneering Blaxploitation film "Sweet Sweetback's Badasssss Song" just before their move to Columbia Records, where they produced the albums "Last Days and Time", "Head To The Sky", and "Open Our Eyes".

It was the soundtrack to an ill-fated film that really marked the beginning of success for Earth Wind & Fire. The film "That's The Way Of The World" was a complete failure at the box office, but the soundtrack produced by Earth Wind & Fire sold huge numbers at the record stores. From this double platinum selling album, Earth, Wind & Fire scored their first number one single with "Shining Star", and won their first Grammy Award. The follow-up albums "Gratitude", "Spirit" and "All 'n All" succeeded in making Earth, Wind & Fire superstars. The group also had a string of hit singles with "Can't Hide Love", "Gratitude", "Fantasy", "Getaway", and a cover of The Beatles' "Got To Get You Into My Life".

These were followed by "The Best Of Earth, Wind & Fire, Vol. 1", "I Am", "Faces", "Raise", and "Powerlight". Which produced the hit singles "September", "Boogie Wonderland", "After The Love Has Gone", "In The Stone", and "Let's Groove".

For their now legendary live performances, Earth Wind & Fire hired magicians Doug Henning and his assistant David Copperfield, to design their stage shows. Band members levitated, flew, disappeared, emerged from pyramids and space ships, drum sets flipped upside down, blinding explosions shook the arenas and whirling lights and lasers dazzled the crowds.

Earth, Wind & Fire perfected their stage choreography while masterfully playing their instruments. The band was always outfitted in lavish costumes, and wore magnificently colored African outfits, sequined metallic futuristic spacesuits, and of course spandex. They were the first to bring Africanized cultural elements into a large-scale pop music performance; even Maurice's trademark instrument was a handheld thumb-played Kalimba from Africa.

In the 1970s, Maurice wrote and produced hits by Ramsey Lewis, Deniece Williams and The Emotions. In 1983, Earth, Wind & Fire took a break after nearly twelve years of non-stop recording and performing. During the break, Maurice released a successful solo album and produced albums for Barbara Streisand and Neil Diamond. Verdine produced an album for the British band Level 42, and Philip recorded a Grammy winning gospel album, and had a international hit single with the duet "Easy Lover" with Phil Collins.

In 1988, Earth Wind & Fire reunited with the album "Touch The World", which produced the hit single "System of Survival". A second volume of greatest hits followed, and in 1994, Earth Wind & Fire released the hit album "Millennium", which earned them a Grammy nomination for the single "Sunday Morning".

In 1996, The Mighty Maurice White made the decision to get off the road after twenty-five years leading one of the greatest bands of all-time. Maurice still produces and sings on Earth, Wind & Fire's recordings, but the band would continue into the next millennium led by Philip and Verdine. Maurice built a state-of-the-art recording studio in Carmel, California, and produced several compelling jazz projects including a pair of all-star "Urban Knights" albums, which feature his old friend Ramsey Lewis collaborating with Grover Washington Jr., Gerald Albright, and Jonathan Butler. He also started a record label called Kalimba Records.

Earth Wind and Fire has won six Grammys Awards, four American

Music Awards and has sold over 20 million albums in the US alone. They have been honored with a star on the Hollywood Walk of Fame, a Hall of Fame Image Award from the NAACP, and on March 6, 2000, Earth, Wind & Fire were inducted into the Rock and Roll Hall of Fame. Without dispute, and in addition, for their uncompromising excellence, prolific catalog of amazing albums and songs, and mind blowing stage spectaculars, Earth Wind & Fire are Rock Music Legends and Icons.

(sources: starpulse.com, earthwindandfire.com, rollingstone.com, theiceberg.com, VH1.com)

GEORGE CLINTON

(Born July 22, 1940, Kannapolis, North Carolina)

The mastermind behind the highly successful Parliament and Funkadelic, George Clinton was born in rural North Carolina. As a child, George's family moved to Plainfield, New Jersey, a mostly African American suburb of Philadelphia. While in junior high school, George formed a five-man doo-wop band called the Parliaments.

After graduating from high school, George and his friends opened a barbershop, where they cut hair in front and rehearsed out back. However, the band found themselves going nowhere in New Jersey, and by the mid 1960s relocated to Detroit landing a deal with Motown rival, Revilot Records. The Parliaments 1967 single "(I Wanna) Testify" reached the top 20, but the band found themselves in a legal dispute with another band called the Parliaments, and were unable to release a follow-up record.

As the legal disputes held up recording, George and his friends began experimenting with their music, adding a full back-up band and becoming fascinated with the growing psychedelic and black power movements. In 1970, the Parliaments changed their name to Parliament, and their backup band became known as Funkadelic. With the addition of keyboard virtuoso Bernie Worell, Funkadelic became a psychedelic band influenced by Jimi Hendrix and the MC5. After the first three albums, the dancibility of the band began to increase.

In 1975, former James Brown saxophonist Maceo Parker and bassist Bootsy Collins, joined the ensemble, stealing thunder from the guitar and keyboards that formally drove Funkadelic. George Clinton would release recordings under both the names Parliament and Funkadelic. Throughout the 1970s the bands co-existed, Funkadelic on Warner Bros. and Parliament on Casablanca, with the entire P-Funk mob splitting their time between recording and touring.

Parliament was more radio-friendly than Funkadelic, but Funkadelic became the more experimental of the two, emphasizing horns and bass rather than guitars, and developing a cartoon-like futuristic image. George Clinton became known as "Dr. Funkenstein", and other band members took equally outrageous names. In, 1976, the group began to mount even more outrageous live shows, most notably landing the huge space craft like flying saucer "The Mother Ship" on stage. Later, in 1977, Parliament scored a number one hit with "Flash Light", and in 1978, Funkadelic scored the number one smash hit "One Nation Under a Groove".

Despite the fact that both Parliament and Funkadelic had several hit albums and singles during the late 1970s, the groups became troubled as key members came and went, and several members including George Clinton himself struggled with drug problems. The expensive costumes and sets that were signatures of the P-Funk shows ate into their profits and they soon found themselves in debt.

By 1981 Parliament and Funkadelic merged into one band, the P-Funk All Stars, which performed less as key members, including George Clinton, concentrated on solo and studio session work. In 1982, George Clinton's first solo album, Computer Games, featured many of the P-Funk musicians, but had a more commercial sound than the Parliament/Funkadelic material. Two singles from the album reached the top of the charts, "Loopzilla" reaching the top 20 and "Atomic Dog" reached number one on the R&B charts in early 1983. George's solo material began to completely break from the P-Funk sound, influenced by rap and electronic sounds. In the late 1980s, George Clinton hooked up with Prince, who paid off George's debts and George Clinton began recording for Prince's label, Paisley Park.

George became more influenced by contemporary music, and began working with groups like the Red Hot Chili Peppers.

In the 1990s, a new generation of young Black musicians and Hip-Hop artist were re-discovering George Clinton's music, and Parliament/Funkadelic records became one of the most frequently sampled sources on rap albums by groups like Ice Cube and Digital Underground. As interest in P-Funk began to grow in the early 1990s, George Clinton and his P-Funk All Stars staged a comeback in 1994 with an appearance at Lollapalooza. The group even brought back the visual spectacle of "The Mother Ship" in 1996. George Clinton and his group continue to record and tour both individually and as The P-Funk All Stars.

In 1997, George Clinton and Parliament/Funkadelic were inducted into the Rock 'N Roll Hall of Fame, paying tribute to years of mind numbing superfunky experimental excellence. In the fall of 1998, at age 58, George Clinton released Dope Dogs, an imaginative concept album about dogs, which included the ultra heavy track, "Dogstar". In 2003, at age 63, George Clinton and his band of P-Funk All-stars are still going strong, touring and bringing his cast of characters and cavalcade of Funketeers to cities and countries all over the world.

George Clinton is an Icon to multiple generations of rock, soul, and funk enthusiast. His innovative and experimental approach to music, production, and performance set the standard for many generations of rockers, rappers, and soulsters to follow. Reflectively, unquestionably, George Clinton and Parliament/Funkadelic are Rock 'N Roll Legends.

(sources: funkvibe.com, theiceberg.com, rollingstone.com, VH1.com)

BOOTSY COLLINS

(Born: October 26, 1951, Cincinnati, Ohio)

William "Bootsy" Collins grew up in Cincinnati, Ohio. As a young teenager, Bootsy along with his brother, guitarist Phelps "Catfish" Collins, formed a band called The Pacemakers, and gained a strong reputation playing gigs at local clubs and bars.

In 1969, they got in touch with James Brown through his production manager Bud Hobgood, and James set them up as studio musicians for different artists. In 1970, James Brown had some internal conflicts with his back-up band, and James' way of handling the situation was to send for the Pacemakers to replace the malcontents. Bobby Byrd called The Pacemakers and told them he would pick them up in James Brown's private jet for a show in Columbus, Georgia, that night.

Bootsy and the group went straight to the show that same night, and without any rehearsal, the Pacemakers went onstage backing up James Brown. Bootsy and The Pacemakers were huge fans of James Brown, and knew all his songs. James called out the songs and the band just played.

Newly dubbed "The JB's", Bootsy and the band stayed with James Brown for nine months, during which time they toured the US, Africa, and Europe. Bootsy and Catfish had a great impact on James Brown's music. A lot of the attention was put on Bootsy's bass and his brother's guitar. They were directly involved in creating some of James Brown's biggest hits, including "Sex Machine", "Soul Power", "Get Up", "Get Into It", "Get Involved" and "Superbad".

James Brown taught Bootsy about funk and about the business of music, but Bootsy was too independent and rebellious to deal with James Brown's control and discipline. While touring in Europe, Bootsy was inspired by the crazy outfits he saw people wearing in nightclubs, and he wanted a project where he could do his own thing, be loose and just have fun. Consequently, Bootsy left James Brown and formed his own group, "The House Guests", who were wild and looked like hippies. Bootsy and The House Guests competed with Funkadelic to be the craziest and loudest group around.

In 1972, the competition took an interesting turn when The House Guests hooked up with George Clinton and Bernie Worell, and eventually merged with Funkadelic. This was Bootsy's first contact with George Clinton and the P-Funk mob. Bootsy still wanted to do his own thing, so he and his former House Guests band members left Funkadelic soon after joining.

Bootsy started writing songs and played on records for various artists, but eventually gravitated back to George Clinton, playing on the Funkadelic perennial "Cosmic Slop". Bootsy and George also collaborated on Parliament's 1974 album "Up For The Down Stroke". Bootsy played the bass on the title track, and in 1975, his contributions increased even more with the album "Chocolate City", on which Bootsy co-wrote five songs.

Bootsy Collins eventually became one of the front men in Parliament, and was a big part of its success. Later that year everything exploded when the hit album "Mothership Connection" was released. The groundbreaking album took the P-Funk mob to the top of the charts and international stardom.

Appreciating Bootsy's wild style and stage presence, George Clinton had for some time been encouraging Bootsy to front a band of his own. So, George got Bootsy a deal with Warner Bros. Records, and together they wrote new songs and put together a backing band which included brother Catfish on guitar, Gary "Mudbone" Cooper, Robert Johnson, and Leslyn Bailey on vocals, Fredrick Allen on keyboards, and Frankie Waddy on drums. Saxophonist Maceo Parker, trombonist Fred Wesley, and trumpeter Rick Garder, formed Bootsy's now infamous Horny Horns horn section, and the group was dubbed "Bootsy's Rubber Band".

The newly formed band gained a strong reputation opening up for Parliament/Funkadelic on the "Earth" tour. Their debut album "Stretchin' Out In Bootsy's Rubber Band" was released in 1976, and Bootsy's new band soon became known as the coolest P-Funk spin-off act. Of course, George Clinton was all over the Rubber Band's production, and probably had a major influence on their "Parliament/Funkadelic-like" concepts.

Reflectively, in 1977, it was George Clinton that came up with The Pinocchio Theory: "*If you fake the funk, your nose gots to grow*" for Bootsy's second album "Ahh... The Name Is Bootsy, Baby!". In 1978, Bootsy's Rubber Band was very successful, and scored a hit single with "Bootzilla".

In 1980, Bootsy and George released Bootsy's fifth album "Ultra Wave", and Bootsy took his new group "Sweat Band" on the road with him to support George's next tour. In 1982, Bootsy recorded his last album for Warner Bros. with "The One Giveth, The Count Taketh Away". Even though Bootsy still worked as a studio musician for George Clinton and Herbie Hancock, this album was his last solo project for six years.

In 1988, Bootsy returned with "What's Bootsy Doin'?", and in 1989, Bootsy was a member of the "Bootzilla Orchestra" on the Malcolm McLaren album "Waltz Dancing". Bootsy entered the 1990s in grand style, scoring a number hit with his super funky bass playing on the smash dance single "Groove Is The Heart" by Dee-Lite. Bootsy continued, releasing his own "Jungle Bass" in 1990, "Blasters Of The Universe" in 1994, and "Fresh Outta P University" in 1997.

Onward into the new millennium the mighty William "Bootsy" Collins went, being celebrated by his contemporaries, his millions of fans, and legions of loyal worshipers from a new generation of flamboyant superstars, that all look up to the mighty Bootzilla baby! Unquestionably, William "Bootsy" Collins is a Funk soldier, a Funk pioneer, and a Funk genius. Bootsy is Funk personified, and an incomparable Rock 'N Roll/Funk Icon.

(sources: yahoo.com, funkvibe.com, theiceberg.com, VH1.com, rollingstone.com)

THE COMMODORES

(Featuring Lionel Richie)

The Commodores were formed at the Tuskegee Institute in Tuskegee, Alabama, in 1968. The band included Lionel Richie on keyboards, saxophone, and vocals, Thomas McClary on guitar, William King on trumpet, Michael Gilbert on bass, Milan Williams on keyboards, and Andre Callahan on drums. Before the Commodores moved to New York in 1969, Andre Callahan and Michael Gilbert were replaced by Walter "Clyde" Orange on drums and Ronald LaPread on bass.

In New York the Commodores became established as a strong club act, specializing in funk instrumentals. In 1970, they recorded the "Rise Up" album for Atlantic Records, which included instrumental cover versions of popular R&B hits, and some original material. In 1972, they secured a support slot on the Jackson 5 American tour. As a result of this, the Commodores signed to Motown Records and toured with the Jackson 5 for three years. In 1975, they earned a support slot on the Rolling Stones US tour. The Commodores became well known for their hard-edged funk songs and ballads written and sung by Lionel Richie. The Commodores scored their first US hit with the instrumental single "Machine Gun", followed by "Slippery When Wet".

Between 1975 and 1977, The Commodores continued to score hits with Lionel Richie's romantic ballads, including "Sweet Love", "Just To Be Close To You" and "Easy". The ultra funky "Too Hot To Trot" and "Brick House" were a return to The Commodores hard-edge funk sound, but by this time, they were increasingly regarded as a soft-soul group. This was emphasized when Lionel Richie's love song, "Three Times A Lady", became a number one smash hit in the US and UK. The touching single is Motown Records biggest selling record to date. The Commodores next single, "Sail On", was also a smash hit, and Lionel Richie began to receive requests to write material for other popular artists.

In 1979, the single "Still" gave The Commodores another pop and soul number one hit, and they became Motown's best-selling group of the 1970s. In 1980, The Commodores tried moving in a funkier direction on the album "Heroes", but it was a commercial failure. The success of Lionel Richie's hit duet "Endless Love", with Diana Ross, resolved Lionel to begin a solo career separate of The Commodores.

The Commodores were crippled by Lionel Richie's departure, and though they continued to perform, they never regained the success they achieved with Lionel. In 1982, the success of "Endless Love" inspired Lionel Richie to release his hit debut solo single, "Truly", which many felt was a continuation of the ballad style Lionel started with The Commodores. In 1983, Lionel Richie released the album "Can't Slow Down", for which he achieved individual superstardom. The album sold more than 15 million copies worldwide, and won two Grammy Awards, including Album of the Year. The album included the number one hit single "All Night Long", which also spawned a hit video, and the top ten hit "Hello". Next, Lionel wrote the hit single "Say You, Say Me", the theme song for the movie "White Nights", which won Lionel Richie an Academy Award. He also collaborated on the charity single "We Are The World" by USA for Africa. In 1986, Lionel released the hit album and single "Dancing on the Ceiling"; the title song was accompanied by another hit music video.

In the 1990s, Lionel Richie didn't enjoy much commercial success, though media attention from a domestic dispute with his wife kept the reclusive artist in an unwanted spotlight. In 1996, Lionel Richie released the album "Louder Than Words", an album of well-crafted music which conformed to an urban R&B sound. The album "Time" featured several of Lionel's trademark ballads and "Renaissance" initially only available in Europe, included more dance driven singles.

As for The Commodores, in 1984, guitarist Thomas McClary launched a solo career with an album for Motown, and JD Nicholas, formerly of the group Heatwave, replaced him. In 1985, The Commodores scored a hit with the single "Nightshift", a tribute to Marvin Gaye and Jackie Wilson. Later that same year, The Commodores left Motown for Polydor Records, prompting bassist Ronald LaPread to leave the band. In 1986, The Commodores scored another hit with the single "Goin' To The Bank", but this single would be their last hit. In 1988, The Commodores' name returned to the UK singles charts when the late 1970s single "Easy", which was used for a television commercial, reached number fifteen.

Even though The Commodores have lost much of their standing as one of America's most popular funk and R&B bands, they will always be respected as one of the greatest recording groups of all times, and a Legendary Rock 'N Roll Band.

(sources: MTV.com, VH1.com, rollingstone.com, lionelrichie.com)

THE OHIO PLAYERS

The Ohio Players were formed in Dayton, Ohio, in 1959 as the Ohio Untouchables, a R&B studio session band. Led by vocalist Leroy "Sugarfoot" Bonner, the group evolved into the Ohio Players, which, by the early 1970s, adopted their trademark funk/rock sound and suave image.

In the 1960s, the Ohio Players recorded for Compass Records. However, when Compass went bankrupt, the band moved over to Capitol Records. In 1968, Capitol Records released the Ohio Players' albums "First Impressions", and "Observations In Time". These recordings stuck to the soul formula of many artists from that time.

In 1970, the group broke up briefly, but in 1971, re-formed and cut the demo "Pain" which got them signed to Westbound Records. The label released the albums "Pain" and "Pleasure" in 1972 and the album "Ecstasy" in 1973. Their first singles hit was the dance track "Funky Worm", which reached the top 20 on the US pop charts. In 1974, The Ohio Players left Westbound and signed with Mercury Records, and the Ohio Players scored a hit with their first album for the Mercury label. The album "Skin Tight" was recorded in only a month, and included the hit singles "Skin Tight" and "Jive Turkey". Also, that same year, the Ohio Players released their ground-breaking hit album "Fire", which went straight to the top of the charts. In 1975, the Ohio Players continued their success with the release of the hit album "Honey". The album included the hit singles "Fopp", "Sweet

Sticky Thing", and the smash hit "Love Rollercoaster".

The Ohio Players were infamous for their risqué album covers, which have included a naked woman holding a fire hose, a naked woman holding a whip, a naked woman tied up in chains and a naked woman covered with honey. It's been said that the idea was to attract male fans with the sexy covers, and attract female fans with the sexy band members. Consequently, the Ohio Players attracted a lot of attention and controversy.

Controversy fueled the bands rise to stardom, and mysterious rumors further kept the band in the public eye. There was the story about the beautiful model who was burned by hot honey during the "Honey" album photo session. The most famous story was that a girl was murdered during the recording of their hit "Love Rollercoaster", and you can hear her screaming in the song. As if concocted by a shrewd promotional campaign, "Love Rollercoaster" became a number one hit on the pop and R&B charts, and the rumors boosted the Ohio Players' record sales and career.

However, the mid 1970s would mark the heyday for the legendary Ohio Players. In the 20 year wake after their international success, the Ohio Players later releases would include the albums "Contradiction" in 1976, "Angel" and "Mr. Mean" in 1977, "Jass-Ay-Lay-Dee" in 1978, "Everybody Up" in 1979. In the 1980s, the Ohio Players released the albums "Tenderness" and "Ouch" in 1981, "Graduation" in 1984, and "Back" in 1988, which scored a minor soul hit with the single "Sweat". In the 1990s, during the retro '70s explosion, the Ohio Players would continue to tour, and released the album "Old School - On Tour" and "Jam 1978 Recording" in 1996.

The Ohio Players set the standard for hard rocking funk bands of that era. Their prolific recording, powerfully sexual album covers, outrageous rumors, and musical talent, made the Ohio Players legends in their own time and Rock 'N Roll Legends today.

(sources: funkvibe.com, rollingstone.com, theiceberg.com, VH1.com)

GIL SCOTT-HERON

(Born: April 1, 1949, Chicago, Illinois)

Gil Scott-Heron was born in Chicago in 1949, where his mother was a librarian and a magna cum laude college graduate, and Gil's father was a professional soccer player from Jamaica. After their divorce, Gil moved in with his grandmother in Lincoln, Tennessee, where young Gil listened to the soul and blues of Memphis.

Gil's grandmother taught him how to play the piano, and in the eighth grade Gil was one of only three Black children to integrate into a local elementary school. However, the cursing and abuse from the White students was too much for young Gil, and he eventually moved to New York City with his mother. It was in a New York City private school that young Gil Scott-Heron first studied the Harlem Renaissance and the poet Langston Hughes.

After high school, Gil enrolled in Lincoln University, in Pennsylvania. However, he dropped out after his freshmen year to concentrate on writing and completed his first novel "The Vulture" and a book of poetry entitled "Small Talk At 125th & Lenox".

In 1970, 21 year old Gil Scott-Heron began working with record producer Bob Thiele. The two blended Gil's politically charged poetry with rhythmic percussion, and recorded Gil Scott-Heron's first album, "Small Talk At 125th & Lenox", named after Gil's book of poetry.

The 1970s ushered in a shift in the struggle for equal rights, as the non-violent movement for civil rights transformed into the highly volatile demand for Black Power. The timing was just right for sharp social-political poetic sound of Gil Scott-Heron.

In 1971, Gil released the album "Pieces Of A Man" and "Free Will" in 1972. 1972 also marked the publishing of Gil's second novel "The Nigger Factory". Gil Scott-Heron was an intelligent, politically minded, strong-willed Black man, speaking out against hypocrisy and the political wrongs perpetrated against Black people, in the pursuit of White happiness.

Gil invented a fresh personalized style of laid back jazzy, soulful grooves, accented by loud rapping and hard beats. Gil Scott-Herons music was unique, and his words would set the tone of revolution in that decade. Further, Gil Scott-Heron was a skillful songwriter whose songs were covered by other artists, including "The Revolution Will Not Be Televised" by LaBelle, and "Home Is Where The Hatred Is" by Esther Phillips.

In 1973, Gil had a minor hit with "The Bottle". In 1975, Gil became the first artist signed to legendary record executive Clive Davis' new record label "Arista Records". With Arista, Gil released the albums, "From South Africa to South Carolina", "Winter In America" and "The First Minute Of A New Day". In 1976, Gil scored a hit with the dance protest single "Johannesburg".

On the 1980s album, "Reflections", Gil recorded a version of Marvin Gaye's "Inner City Blues", but his strongest songs were his own social-political songs that dealt with nuclear power, apartheid and poverty. Gil also focused musical attacks on politicians like Richard Nixon, Gerald Ford, Barry Goldwater, Jimmy Carter, and Ronald Reagan. In 1982, Gil scored a small hit with his anti-Reagan rap, "B-Movie". However by 1985, Gil Scott-Heron was dropped by Arista, just after the release of "The Best of Gil Scott-Heron". Gil continued touring, but didn't release any new material again until the mid 1990's.

In 1994, Gil Scott-Heron signed with TVT Records, and released the album "Spirits", which was met with critical praise. Spirits' first single "Message To The Messengers" was a mandate to modern Hip-Hop artist, urging them to take responsibility for their artistic influence in their communities. Interestingly, soon after, Gil Scott-Heron was recognized as one of the forefathers of modern Hip-Hop, and was featured on CNN, network news, in Rolling Stone, Spin, Vibe, and Musician magazines. Impressively and deservedly, Gil Scott-Heron was getting his due.

With a Masters Degree in Creative Writing from Johns Hopkins University, Gil Scott-Heron the writer, poet, and musician is a true artist. In 2001 he was imprisoned for cocaine possession, and militant to a fault, he turned down rehabilitation as an alternative to prison. He was released from prison on October 28th, 2002.

Gil Scott-Heron is one of the most influential forefathers of Hip Hop music, and his aggressively militant, social-political music and poetry have inspired a legion of intelligent Rock, R&B and Rap artist, making Gil-Scott Heron a Rock 'N Roll Hero and Legend!

(sources: glp.at, theiceberg.com, yahoo.com, home.clara.net)

CURTIS MAYFIELD

(Born: June 3, 1942, Chicago, Illinois)

Curtis Mayfield was born in Chicago, where at an early age he taught himself to play the guitar and developed an innate talent for songwriting.

Curtis Mayfield's first group was "The Alphatones", after which he joined "The Roosters", lead by his friend Jerry Butler from the church choir. The Roosters later became "The Impressions", and in 1958, Curtis dropped out of high school in the ninth grade to record The Impressions' first hit single "For Your Precious Love", on Vee-Jay Records. However, after their success, the label urged Jerry Butler to go solo, and the remaining group members were forced into limbo without a record deal.

Curtis Mayfield had a uniquely delicate voice and a wonderful singing falsetto, and in 1961, led The Impressions to New York and recorded the hit "Gypsy Woman" for ABC/Paramount Records. In the early 1960's, Curtis was a busy songwriter, who wrote songs for Jerry Butler, Major Lance and many others artist.

Curtis was also very busy with The Impressions, releasing successful chart topping records like "It's All Right" in 1963, "I'm So Proud", "Keep On Pushing" and "You Must Believe In Me" in 1964, and the soulful favorite "People Get Ready" in 1965.

Curtis was a smart businessman, and had control over his music publishing. He was also one of the first artist to openly write songs about Black Pride. Curtis and Impressions' manager Eddie Thomas owned Curtom Records, which was very successful from 1968 to 1980. Curtom's roster of acts and artist included "The Staple Singers", "Linda Clifford", "The Natural Four", and "Major Lance".

In the later part of the 1960s, Curtis Mayfield's social-political messages became brazen. Curtis no longer shrouded his messages in metaphors, he became extremely blunt in songs like "We're a Winner" and "This Is My Country" in 1968, and "Mighty Mighty Spade And Whitey" in 1969.

In 1970, Curtis Mayfield left The Impressions and went solo. Later that same year Curtis released his debut solo album entitled "Curtis", which included the singles "(Don't Worry) If There's Hell Below We're All Gonna Go", an unheard of eight-minute psychedelic track. Curtis' next single "Move On Up", was even longer, running nearly nine minutes.

In 1971, Curtis Mayfield released the albums "Roots" and "Curtis Live". Notably, the genre of Blaxploitation films started that same year with Black director Melvin Van Peebles' movie "Sweet Sweetback's Baadasssss Song". 'Blaxploitation' was a new genre of films starring Black people as the heroes, kicking ass, and making love. That next year in 1972, Curtis Mayfield wrote and recorded his biggest album, "Superfly", a complete soundtrack to the now legendary Blaxploitation film "Superfly." "Superfly" was the story of a Harlem cocaine pusher, played by actor Ron O'Neal, with a smooth straight perm. The film glorified the mythical ghetto-fabulous lifestyle of a hip New York player with fancy fly cars and hot sexy women.

Curtis was so inspired by the script that he wrote all new songs to fit the movie. Curtis got funkier than he had been before, and wrote music and lyrics from the characters' point of view. The album was a masterpiece and included the groundbreaking hit singles "Superfly", "Pusherman", and the unforgettable "Freddie's Dead".

Curtis Mayfield wrote and recorded prolifically during the 1970s, releasing one incredible album after another. In addition to his own projects he wrote and produced music for five more films and acts such as Gladys Knight and The Pips, The Staple Singers, and Aretha Franklin.

Keeping with the times, Curtis Mayfield recorded and released the dance albums "Do It All Night" and "Heartbeat". Curtis still focused on social and political messages on the albums "Back To The World" and "There's No Place Like America Today". The album covers' art dawned pictures of Black people in Great Depression soup lines, while a happy White family drives by in a new car.

In the 1980s, the Curtom label shut down. Curtis Mayfield however, continued touring, released four albums on different labels, and made sure to spend plenty of quality time with his children. In 1990, Curtis revived Curtom Records and released his comeback album "Take It To The Streets". He hit the road and recorded music for the Superfly sequel "Return Of Superfly". Then disaster struck. During an August 1990 charity concert in New York, a light rig fell in a windstorm, hitting Curtis. He was rushed to Kings County Hospital where doctors diagnosed him with permanent paralysis from the neck down.

In 1994, Curtis Mayfield received a Grammy Legend Award, and in 1995, he received a Grammy Lifetime Achievement Award. Remarkably, in 1996, a still paralyzed Curtis Mayfield surprised the world, and released a new album called "New World Order", which was nominated for three Grammy Awards. The whole project was a monumental effort, and took a tremendous toll on the ailing legend. Curtis Mayfield died on Sunday, May 26, 1999, at the North Fulton Regional Hospital in Roswell, Georgia. He was 57 years old.

Curtis Mayfield was a Rock 'N Roll Hall of Fame member, A Grammy Award winner, and a musical genius, who dared to be great, and excelled to the pantheon of Rock 'N Roll Legends.

(sources: rhythmandtheblues.org, funkvibe.com, theiceberg.com, VH1.com)

ISAAC HAYES

(Born: August 6, 1942, Covington, Tennessee)

I saac Hayes was born in Covington, Tennessee. Both of his parents died when Isaac was just an infant, and so his grandmother in Memphis raised him. Young Isaac sang in his church choir for years, and didn't start performing secular music until he began playing in his high school band.

Isaac Hayes' professional music career began when he went to work as a session musician with Stax Records, the home of artists like Otis Redding, Wilson Pickett, Sam & Dave, and Booker T. & the MG's. Very quickly, Isaac became the label's most prolific writer and producer of hit songs. In the late 1960s, Isaac Hayes' successful collaboration with David Porter produced a multitude of hits made famous by Sam & Dave. The hits included, "You Don't Know Like I Know", "Hold On, I'm Coming", "You Got Me Hummin'", "When Something is Wrong with My Baby", "I Thank You", "I Take What I Want", "Wrap It Up" and "Soul Man".

In 1967, Isaac Hayes released his debut solo album, entitled "Presenting Isaac Hayes". In 1969, at the peak of the Civil Rights Movement, Isaac released the hit album "Hot Buttered Soul", which included the hit singles "By the Time I Get to Phoenix", and "Walk On By".

Isaac's next album "The Isaac Hayes Movement", went platinum, and his success was only beginning. In 1971, the soundtrack album for the legendary film "Shaft" catapulted Isaac Hayes' career into superstardom. For his effort, Isaac Hayes won an Academy Award, two Grammys, a Golden Globe, the NAACP Image Award, and the album and single were certified platinum. In addition, he began an acting career in the film "Truck Turner and Three Tough Guys". In 1971, Isaac released the hit double platinum, double-album "Black Moses", followed by another double-album, "Live at the Sahara Tahoe", which was certified gold. In 1973, Isaac released the album "Joy", concluding his contractual obligation to Stax Records.

In 1975, Isaac Hayes started his own label "Hot Buttered Soul Records", and released the gold album "Chocolate Chip". Also in 1975, he was featured in the comedy film "It Seemed Like a Good Idea At the Time". Isaac also did television, playing the character "Rockfish" on The Rockford Files. In 1976, Isaac released his final album for his Hot Buttered Soul label, entitled "Groovathon". In 1977, Isaac recorded the album "A Man and A Woman" with Dionne Warwick, featuring the singles "By the Time I Get to Phoenix" and "Say a Little Prayer". Also in 1977, he signed with Polydor Records and produced the album "New Horizon". In 1978, Isaac Hayes released the top ten R&B hit album "Don't Let Go", and In 1979, he released "Royal Rappin's" with Millie Jackson.

Isaac recorded twice more for Polydor, the 1980 album "And Once Again" and 1981's "Lifetime Thing". In the early 1980s, Isaac appeared in the TV series Hunter, Miami Vice, and The A-Team. In 1986, he co-starred with Paul Sorvino in the TV movie "Betrayed By Innocence", and with Ed Marinaro in "The Sofia Conspiracy". Also in 1986, Isaac Hayes released the album "U-Turn", and later that same year, he released the top ten R&B hit single "Ike's Rap/Hey Girl". The single had a strong anti-drug theme, and reportedly caused several addicts to seek rehabilitation. Consequently, Isaac Hayes took his inspirational anti-drug message across the country speaking in colleges and prisons. It was said that a rehab-center in Detroit, Michigan, even used Isaac's lyric "Don't be a resident of crack city", as a sweatshirt slogan. Afterward, Isaac released the album "Love Attack", on which he produced, wrote, and played most of the instruments. In 1988, he co-starred in the Keenan Ivory Wayans' comedy "I'm Gonna Git You Sucka".

In 1992, Isaac Hayes became the international spokesman for the World Literacy Crusade, in which he spoke to people everywhere about the possibility of future hope, higher education, and worthwhile employment without the need for guns or violence. In 1993, Isaac appeared in Mel Brooks' comedy "Robin Hood: Men in Tights", and in 1996, Isaac released two albums "Branded" and "Raw and Refined", as well as co-writing the soundtrack to the animated film "Beavis & Butthead Do America".

Isaac Hayes was featured on a host of film soundtracks in the 1990s. Amazingly, Isaac Hayes' sexy voice and persona propelled him to contemporary cult icon, when he signed on to be the voice of the ultra sexy "Chef", on the wildly popular animated television series South Park. The "Chef" character endeared the mighty Isaac Hayes to a whole new generation of fans and admirers. In 1998, "Chef Aid: The South Park Album", was certified platinum, and Isaac appeared on four of the album's tracks, scoring a number one hit in the UK with the single "Chocolate Salty Balls". In 1999, a South Park film was released, also featuring the voice of Isaac Hayes as the lovable Chef. In addition, since its release, "Chef Aid: The South Park Album" has gone gold in the United Kingdom, triple platinum in Canada, triple platinum in Australia, and is almost double-platinum in the US. Isaac Hayes had become a multi-generational superstar.

Isaac Hayes was the first African American to win an Oscar for Best Musical Score, and for forty years, he has embodied the very essence of soul. His bald, bearded, body wrapped in gold chains, his brilliant soundtracks, and sexy voice, personify musical sensuality. In addition to his musical genius, Isaac Hayes' humanitarian efforts in Africa and the United States, make him a shinning example of an International Rock 'N Roll Icon!

(sources: rollingstone.com, isaachayes.com, funkvibe.com, VH1.com)

AL GREEN

(Born: April 13, 1946, Forrest City, Arkansas)

Al Green was born in Forest City, Arkansas, where he formed a gospel quartet, "The Green Brothers", at the age of nine. The group toured throughout the South in the 1950s, before his family relocated to Grand Rapids, Michigan. The Green Brothers continued to perform in Grand Rapids, but Al's father made Al leave the group after he caught him listening to Jackie Wilson records.

In 1962, at the age of 16, Al Green formed the R&B group, "Al Green and the Creations", with some high school friends. Two of the Creations' members started their own record label, Hot Line Music Journal, and had the group record for them. By then, the Creations were re-named the "Soul Mates", and their first single was "Back Up Train", which became a surprise hit in 1968. The Soul Mates attempted to record another hit, but all of their subsequent singles failed.

In 1969, Al Green signed a deal with Hi Records and began recording his debut album. In 1970, Al Green's debut album "Green is Blues" showcased his signature sound highlighted by Al Green's remarkable falsetto, super sexy horns and the Hammond B-3 organ. Also in 1970, Al released "Al Green Gets Next To You", which included his first hit single, "Tired of Being Alone". This began a streak of four straight gold hit singles including "Let's Stay Together" in 1972, "Look What You Done For Me", "I'm Still In Love With You", and the perinial album favorite "Love and Happiness". In 1973, Al Green's hits continued over the next two years with the top ten gold singles

"Call Me", "Here I Am", and "Sha-La-La".

In 1974, at the height of his popularity, Al Green's personal life was rocked. Following an argument, his girlfriend Mary Woodson burst in while he was taking a bath and poured boiling grits over his back. She then shot herself dead with his gun. Al interpreted the incident as a sign from God to enter the ministry, and in 1976, The Reverend Al Green bought a church in Memphis and had become an ordained pastor of the Full Gospel Tabernacle. Though he practiced his religion seriously, he had not given up singing R&B and released three more albums "Al Green Is Love" in 1975, and "Full of Fire" and "Have A Good Time" in 1976.

In 1977, he built his own American Music studio to produce his own records, "The Belle Album" in 1977, and "Truth and Time" in 1978. In 1979, during a concert in Cincinnati, Ohio, he fell off stage and injured himself. Interpreting the accident as another sign from God, Al Green retired from performing secular music and devoted himself to preaching full-time.

Throughout the 1980s, Al Green released a series of Gospel albums, and in 1982, he appeared in the gospel musical "Your Arms Too Short to Box with God" with Patti LaBelle. In 1985, Al released "He Is the Light", his first album for A&M Records. He tentatively returned to R&B in 1988 when he sang "Put A Little Love In Your Heart" with Annie Lennox for the movie comedy "Scrooged".

In 1991, he recorded his first secular soul album since 1978 with the UK release "Don't Look Back". In 1995, he released "Your Heart's In Good Hands", his first secular album in America since Truth and Time.

Al Green has remained primarily a religious performer for the past 25 years of his career. Nevertheless, his classic early recordings retained their power and influence through the decades, setting the standard for smooth soul singing, with a legendary voice that no one could ever forget. The Reverend Al Green is a Rock 'N Roll Legend!

(sources: zoo.co.uk, rollingstone.com, theiceberg.com, yahoo.com, rhythmandtheblues.org)

BARRY WHITE

(Born: September 12, 1944, Galveston, Texas)

B arry White was born in Galveston, Texas, but was raised in Los Angeles, California. A young musical prodigy, Barry White played piano on Jesse Belvin's hit, "Goodnight My Love", at the age of 11.

As a teenager in the 1960s, Barry made several records as Barry Lee, and he made his first record when he was 16-years old with a group called the "Upfronts". The Upfronts recorded the single "Little Girl" on Lummtone Records. Later Barry White worked for various other record labels around the Los Angeles area, eventually landing an Artist Relations (A&R) job with Bob Keene, who first recorded Sam Cooke.

In 1966, Barry White was hired at $40 a week to do A&R for Bob Keene's labels, Mustang and Bronco Records, and made a record for Bronco called "All in the Run of a Day". However Barry gave priority to his A&R duties. One of the first groups Barry worked with was the "Versatiles" who later became the "5th Dimension". Barry White's first big hit came with Viola Wills' single "Lost Without the Love of My Guy", which went Top twenty on the R&B charts. Consequently, Barry's salary increased to $60 a week.

After that, Barry started working with Bob Keene's big act "The Bobby Fuller Four". The label was also interested in recording a female act. Barry thought of a singer named Felice Taylor, and they produced three big hit singles, "It May Be Winter Outside", "I'm Under the Influence of Love", and "I Feel Love Coming On". As a result of such a huge success, Barry White started making $400 a week.

However , eventually Bronco Records went out of business, and Barry struggled, doing independent production when he could. A compliment to his character, Barry White had true and loyal friends who helped him out, and gave him work and loans during these lean times. It was during this time that Barry started working with the girl-group "Love Unlimited", and he wrote "Walkin' in the Rain" inspired by conversations with one of the group's singers.

After three years of struggling, Barry White was contacted by former business associates and recorded an album for Uni/MCA Records. Love Unlimited's "From a Girl's Point of View" became a million selling album. However, soon after the success, Barry White's relationship with Uni/MCA became strained, but Love Unlimited was still contractually bound to the label. In his frustration, Barry decided to work on a male act. Barry made a three song demo of himself singing and playing the piano, and it was so good that he re-record and released them under his own name. The record became the first Barry White album, 1973s "I've Got So Much to Give", released on 20th Century Records, and showcased his now legendary super sexy baritone voice and big-man appeal.

Barry White got Love Unlimited released from their contract at Uni/MCA, and they joined him at 20th Century. He then had an idea for an instrumental album. Barry wanted to call it the "Love Unlimited Orchestra". The Love Unlimited Orchestra was a forty-piece ensemble, which Barry conducted, composed and arranged. The single, "Love's Theme", was a million selling, number one pop hit and a smash worldwide. The song earned Barry White a BMI award for over three million copies sold.

Barry White recorded several more gold albums, including "Stone Gon'", "Just Another Way to Say I Love You", "Barry White Sings for Someone You Love", "The Man", and the hit album "Can't Get Enough", which featured the smash hit singles "You're the First, the Last, My Everything," and "Can't Get Enough of Your Love, Babe". Barry also produced a soundtrack for the 20th Century Fox film "The Together

Brothers", and was so popular during the 1970s, that Dinah Shore devoted a full hour of her daily TV show to Barry and his music.

Barry White's studio band included guitarists Ray Parker Jr., bassist Nathan East, Wah Wah Watson, Dean Parks, Don Peake, bassist Wilton Felder of the Crusaders, guitarist Lee Ritenour, drummer Ed Greene, percussionist Gary Coleman, and keyboardist Rahn Coleman. With this all-star team in place, by the end of the 1970s, Barry White had produced 22 albums and scored the additional hit singles "It's Ecstasy When You Lay Down Next to Me" and "Let the Music Play".

Barry took 18 months off in 1983, but returned to the charts in the mid 1980s, with the hits "I Wanna Do It Good to Ya" and "Sho You Right". After Barry White released Love Unlimited Orchestra's "My Musical Bouquet" and his own "I Love to Sing the Songs I Sing", Barry left 20th Century and signed a custom label deal with CBS Records. Barry White started the label "Unlimited Gold Records", whose artists included Barry White, Love Unlimited, the Love Unlimited Orchestra, Jack Perry, and teenage singer Danny Pearson who charted with the single "What's Your Sign Girl".

In 1992, Barry White signed with A&M Records, and released the albums "The Man Is Back", "The Right Night Barry White", and "Put Me in Your Mix", which included the duet "Dark and Lovely" with Isaac Hayes. Barry White's next album "The Icon Is Love" became his biggest-selling album of the 1990s, going multi-platinum, and including the platinum selling hit single "Practice What You Preach". Barry followed it up with the album "Staying Power", in 1999. Sadly, in 2003, at the age of 58, Barry White died, after a heroic battle with long-term illness. He will be missed.

Barry White's career took him from obscurity to international success with 106 gold albums, 41 platinum albums, 20 gold singles, 10 platinum singles, and worldwide sales in excess of 100 million units. Barry White, was an American Treasure, a musical legend, and will always be the Rock 'N Roll Icon of Love.

(sources: rollingstone.com, funkvibe.com, theiceberg.com, yahoo.com, VH1.com)

THE BROTHERS JOHNSON

The Brothers Johnson, George, born May 17, 1953, and Louis born April 13, 1955, grew up in Los Angeles. They were still in school when they put together the band "Johnson Three Plus One" along with another brother, Tommy, and their cousin Alex Weir.

Guitarist George Johnson and bassist Louis Johnson were very talented musicians, who got to work with well-known soul acts at an early age. They played in the backing bands of The Supremes, Bobby Womack, and in the early 1970s they were recruited by Billy Preston, and wrote the singles "Music in My Life" and "The Kids and Me", before leaving Billy's group in 1973.

Louis Johnson was a highly skilled bass player, and appeared on albums by Herbie Hancock, Grover Washington Jr., Bill Withers, and Bobby Womack. In 1975, Producer Quincy Jones was so impressed by The Brothers Johnson, that he asked them to play on his "Mellow Madness" album. Quincy recorded four songs written by The Brothers Johnson, including "Is It Love That We're Missing?" and "Just a Taste of Me". The brothers also joined Quincy on his tours through the US and Japan.

In 1976, The Brothers Johnson band was formed, Quincy Jones signed them to A&M Records and produced their debut album "Look Out For # 1". The album catapulted the group straight to stardom, with the number one single "I'll Be Good To You", and the dance classic "Get The Funk Out Ma Face". The Brothers Johnson and

Quincy Jones worked together for four albums. Their second album "Right On Time", released in 1977, sold gold in just three days. The album included the worldwide hit "Strawberry Letter 23". The Brother's Johnson third album "Blam!" didn't have a hit single, but they compensated on the fourth album "Light Up The Night", which included the hit single "Stomp".

In 1981, The Brothers Johnson released their self-produced album "Winners", which included the hit singles "The Real Thing" and "Welcome to the Club". In 1982, Louis Johnson worked with Quincy Jones on Michael Jackson's 40 million selling monster album "Thriller". In 1984, The Brothers Johnson released their sixth album "Out Of Control", which included the hit single "You Keep Coming Back", and in 1988, The Brothers Johnson released their last album "Kickin'", achieving a minor hit with the single "Kick It To The Curb".

The Brothers Johnson are a shining example of excellence in multi-talented musicianship and super sexy soulful and funky songwriting. The Brothers Johnson will always be remembered by music fans as Rock 'N Roll Heroes.

(sources: rollingstone.com, funkvibe.com, theiceberg.com, yahoo.com,VH1.com)

BILLY PRESTON

(Born: September 2, 1946, Houston, Texas)

Billy Preston was born in Houston, Texas, but later moved to Los Angeles, California. Billy began playing piano at age three, and at seven he won a contest in elementary school to direct the Houston Symphony Orchestra. He directed "The Voices of Victory", the 100 person choir from Victory Baptist Church, were his mother played the piano. Billy played the organ even though his feet couldn't reach the foot pedals!

At the age of ten, Billy Preston was performing with gospel legend, Mahalia Jackson, and by twelve, he made his first movie appearance as the young W.C. Handy in "St. Louis Blues". In 1960, Billy Preston played with such gospel stars as The Reverend James Cleveland and The Staple Singers. Billy's first rock 'n roll tour was with Little Richard in Europe. Sam Cooke, who Billy knew from his gospel touring, was also on the tour. After Europe, Billy signed with Sam Cooke's SAR/Derby Records.

Billy Preston's debut album was "The 16 Year Old Soul", and he first met and became good friends with the Beatles during the tour to promote his album. In 1966, Billy Preston charted for the first time with "The Most Exciting Organ Ever", an instrumental gospel album on Vee Jay Records. Billy was also a regular performer on the TV series "The Shindig" for ABC-TV. On the show, Billy Preston showed off his talents as both a pianist and singer. During this time, Billy also built a reputation as a hot session musician. On the TV show, Billy

Preston met his idol Ray Charles, and recorded and toured with Ray for three years. When Billy toured the UK with Ray Charles, he hooked up with George Harrison of the Beatles, and the Beatles decided to buy Billy's recording contract from Vee Jay and sign him to their own label, Apple Records.

Billy Preston had a hit in the UK with "That's The Way God Planned It", produced by George Harrison, and the following year Billy performed at the legendary Concert For Bangladesh. It's been said that Billy Preston is acknowledged as the Fifth Beatle, because of his work on The Beatles recordings "Let It Be", "Abbey Road" and "White Album". Notably, Billy Preston is the only musician to ever have full album credits with the Beatles. Billy Preston also appeared with them in the films, "Let It Be" and "The Complete Beatles", and it was Billy Preston who performed with them during final rooftop concert.

In the late 1960s, Billy Preston worked with John Lennon and Yoko Ono on their album "Plastic Ono Band", and Billy Preston played the title character, Sgt. Pepper, and performed the song "Get Back", in the Beatles tribute film "Sgt. Pepper's Lonely Hearts Club Band".

In the early 1970s, Billy Preston scored number one hit singles with the Grammy winning "Outa Space", "Will It Go Round In Circles", "Nothing From Nothing", and "Space Race". A prolific writer, Billy Preston wrote the multi-platinum selling hit "You Are So Beautiful", made famous by British singing legend Joe Cocker. Billy Preston also performed with Sly and The Family Stone and on the Rolling Stones 1975 US tour.

In 1980, Billy appeared in the movie "The Blues Brothers", and in 1989, Billy toured in his old Beatles friend Ringo Starr's All Star Band. However, like many of his contemporaries, Billy Preston had his bouts with substance abuse and run-ins with the law. In 1991, Billy Preston was arrested on a morals charge, and in 1997, he was sentenced to three years for drug possession. But apparently this goes with the territory, and in no way detracts from the genius of the man, or the monumental accomplishment of his career.

Billy Preston is a multi-platinum selling, Grammy Award winning, Rock 'N Roll Hall of Fame member, who has collaborated with the music industries top artist, including The Beatles, Sammy Davis Jr., Aretha Franklin, Sly Stone, The Jackson Five, Quincy Jones, The Rolling Stones, Barbara Striesand, and U2. Deservingly, Billy Preston will always be remembered as a great musician, songwriter, and highly regarded Rock 'N Roll Hero!

(sources: rollingstone.com, billypreston.net, jcchorus.com, theiceberg.com, VH1.com)

SLY STONE

(Born: March 15, 1944, Dallas, Texas)

Sylvester Stewart was born in Texas, however, the Stewart family soon moved to Vallejo, California, a suburb near San Francisco. Young Sylvester loved to sing in church, and learned to play guitar when he was nine years old. Sylvester's whole family was musically gifted, and he and his siblings formed the group Stewart Four.

In 1962, Sylvester finished high school, and enrolled at Solano Community College to study music theory. He also studied radio broadcasting and engineering at the Chris Borden School of Modern Broadcasting. While in school, Sylvester was in a group called "The Viscaynes", who recorded the single "Yellow Moon". The owners of Autumn Records, seeing Sly's talent, signed Sly as a songwriter and producer. In 1963, at 19 years old, Sylvester got his first big hit when singer Bobby Freeman recorded Sly's song "C'mon And Swim". Sly produced and played most of the instruments in the studio and the single went gold. During this exciting period, Sylvester was also a DJ at Bay Area radio station KSOL, where he was know for being a cool on-air personality, and it was around this time that Sylvester Stewart began calling himself "Sly Stone".

Around 1966, Sly put together a band called "Sly and The Stoners", and at night, as soon as he got off the air at KSOL, Sly would go directly to a club to play gigs with the Stoners. However, Sly felt that some of the band wasn't taking the gigs and his music seriously, so, Sly began looking for a new group of musicians. Sly's brother Freddie was playing guitar with his band "Freddie and The Stone Souls", and Sly heard about a great bass player named Larry Graham. Sly recruited Freddie, and went down to a club to see this bass player. At the club, Sly saw that Larry Graham had a powerful bass playing style. Larry's group didn't have a drummer, so, to make up for it, Larry played his bass by "slapping", "plucking", and "thumping" the strings. Impressed by Larry Graham's ability, Sly asked Larry to join the band.

The new band was Sly on vocals and keyboards, Sly's brother Freddie on guitar, Cynthia Robinson on trumpet, Jerry Martini on saxophone, Sly's sister Rosie on piano, Larry Graham on bass and Gregg Errico on drums. With his new band, which he dubbed "Sly and The Family Stone", Sly created something special. Sly's concept for the band was a mixture of races, genders, and cultures. Sly also wanted something spectacular, and all the band members were sent to the North Beach Leather store in San Francisco, were they picked out any outfit they wanted for free. Their first gig was at a club called Winchester Cathedral, and they became regulars there, playing until early in the morning on most nights. The band played specially ar-ranged covers, and in a short time their crowds got really big, and soon Sly and the Family were well known.

Sly and the band always started the show by having one member at a time take the stage. First onstage was the drummer, who would lay the beat down. Then each member of the band would come onstage and begin to play, until last, but not least, Sly would take the stage and the party would begin. An executive from Epic Records heard about the bands performances at Winchester Cathedral and after seeing them perform, signed the band to a record contract. After signing the deal, Sly and the band went to Las Vegas where they played at Pussycat à Go Go, triumphantly repeating their success.

While they played in Las Vegas, they slowly began incorporating their own songs into their performances, and once a week the band flew from Las Vegas to Los Angeles to record their debut album. In 1967, the album "A Whole New Thing" was released on Epic Records.

The recording was a hard and intense mix of rock, soul, and funk. However, the album sold poorly, and soon after, the band left Las Vegas for New York.

In 1968, The band was performing at Electric Circus, and of course, packing the place. However, Sly was still bitter over the poor sales of his debut album, and began recording a more accessible pop album. The result was the smash hit album "Dance To The Music", which included the hit single of the same name. The song is arranged the way the band used to come on stage, one instrument at a time. The success of "Dance To The Music" allowed the band to play larger venues, and they quickly became famous from radio play and appearances on television shows.

They played four gigs at The Fillmore East, opening for Jimi Hendrix. During the shows, and with the band still playing, Sly, Freddie, and Larry, would march off stage, into the crowd, go out the exit, and into the street, followed by the amazed crowd. After jamming on the sidewalk, Sly would then lead the crowd back inside, and continue the performance. Later that same year, "Dance To The Music" was followed by another strong album entitled "Life".

It was the Sly and The Family Stone album "Stand!" that would make them famous beyond their widest dreams. In 1969, Sly and the Family released the super hit album "Stand", which included the smash hit single "Everyday People". The single was considered by many to be a groundbreaking song, which tackled the subjects of racial and social acceptance in a still bitterly divided country. In support of their hit album and single, the band toured and played various festivals, and when they appeared at Newport Jazz Festival they caused a riot with their incredible stage show. It's been said that the show was sold out, but there were still 30,000 people outside trying to get in, and during the song "You Can Make It If You Try", the mob outside crashed the gates, rushed the stage, and destroyed everything in sight, including the tour bus.

Typically, drugs had been around the group since the beginning, but their use of marijuana and cocaine had increased over time to mythical proportions. In 1968, on a promotional tour of England, Larry Graham was busted by customs for marijuana possession.

In 1969, the pinnacle of Sly and the Family Stone's career was Woodstock. They didn't get on stage until 3.30am, and had to literally wake up the crowd. It took a couple of songs before the crowd got to their feet, but when they did, Sly and The Family Stone had almost half a million people dancing to their music. Also in 1969, the band released the hit single "Hot Fun In The Summertime", which showed off a softer side of Sly and the band.

In 1970, they released the smash hit single, "Thank You (Falettinme Be Mice Elf Agin)", which introduced the world to Larry Graham's unique way of playing, because the bass guitar was turned up and put out front. Since then, the slapping thumping bass line has become a mainstay in funk music. In 1971, the band released the hit album "There's A Riot Going On", which produced the band's biggest hit single ever, the number one smash "Family Affair". In 1973, the album "Fresh", was released by Sly and The Family Stone. This was ironic because even though the album cover said "Sly And The Family Stone", it was almost a one-man performance by Sly, who had hidden himself away in his home studio plagued by an ever-increasing drug habit.

Sadly, in the early 1970s, Sly and Freddie started hanging out with an even faster crowd, and heavier drug use followed. It was said, that Sly transformed from a kind, charming intellectual, into a confused self-absorbed junkie who developed stage fright and paranoia, and Freddie also changed for the worse.

Sly became infamous for arriving late to shows, or not showing up at all, and from 1970 to 1971, he failed to perform at 38 out of 120 shows, causing riots at some venues. Sly's erratic behavior eventually led to concert promoters not wanting to risk booking the band. Original band members Gregg and Larry left the group between the albums Riot and Fresh, because drugs had turned Sly into an unpleasant person. They were replaced by musicians Rusty Allen and Andy

Newmark. Jerry also left, and was replaced by Pat Rizzo; however, Jerry had a change of heart and Sly kept both sax players.

In 1974, Sly married his girlfriend Kathleen in rockstar fashion. The ceremony took place onstage in front of 20,000 people at New York's Madison Square Garden. They had the reception at the ultra posh Waldorf Astoria hotel. The press and many celebrities attended, giving Sly lots of great publicity. Sadly, Sly's marriage to Kathleen Silva ended six months after the wedding.

Sly and The Family Stone's next albums, "Small Talk" in 1974, and "High On You" in 1975, didn't chart and this time the band completely broke up in 1975. Sly continued to record alone, releasing "Heard Ya Missed Me, Well I'm Back" in 1976, and "Back On The Right Track" in 1979. However, none of these albums achieved any commercial success. Sly briefly joined up with George Clinton, performing on, and touring in support of the Funkadelic album "The Electric Spanking of War Babies", but Sly purposely stayed out of the spotlight.

In 1982, Sly Stone released his last album "Ain't But The One Way", and summarily withdrew from recording, only appearing on some duets in the 1980s. In 1983, Sly was arrested for cocaine possession, and entered a drug treatment program. Sadly, he never quite recovered, and drifted in and out of prison and rehab for the remainder of the decade. In 1993, Sly came out of seclusion to appear at Sly and The Family Stone's induction to the Rock and Roll Hall of Fame, but afterward, the mysterious Sly Stone disappeared completely from the public eye.

Regardless of his legendary eccentric behaviors, Sly Stone was unquestionably a visionary songwriter, producer, and performer, who is still respected and emulated to this day. Sly's vision for a multicultural, racially mixed musical group paved the way for generations of rock 'n roll bands to come. Sly Stone was a genius, and a bonafied Rock 'N Roll Legend.

(sources: rollingstone.com, funkvibe.com, theiceberg.com, yahoo.com, VH1.com)

CAMEO

Cameo was originally formed in 1976, as a 13 piece band called the "New York City Players", founded by Juliard educated frontman Larry Blackmon. After changing the name to "Cameo", the band recorded their first single "Find My Way", which lead to a deal with Casablanca Records.

In 1977, Cameo signed with Casablanca subsidiary label Chocolate City Records, the same label as George Clinton and Parliament, and Larry Blackmon produced Cameo's debut album, "Cardiac Arrest". Cameo consequently toured with label-mates Parliament and Funkadelic, to promote their new album.

In 1978, Cameo released the album "We All Know Who We Are", and called their music "C-Funk" (possibly because Parliament called its music "P-Funk"). Also later that same year, the band released the album "Ugly Ego". Cameo's first three albums produced heavy funk hits like "Rigor Mortis", "Funk Funk", "C On The Funk", "Inflation", "Insane" and "Ugly Ego".

In 1979, Cameo released their fourth album "Secret Omen", which went gold. As did "Feel Me" and "Cameosis" in 1980, "Knights of the Sound Table" in 1981, and the hard rocking "Alligator Woman" in 1982. Cameo transitioned beautifully into the 1980s, and in 1983, Larry Blackmon started his own record company Atlanta Artists Label, moved Cameo over to his new label and released the album "Style".

In 1984, Cameo had a number one R&B hit with the single "She's Strange", which crossed over into the pop market, and in 1985 Cameo struck gold again with the hit song "Single Life". In 1986, Cameo released their international hit album "Word Up", which included the number one hit single of the same name ("Word Up") and the smash hit "Candy". That year bandleader Larry Blackmon also attracted a lot of media attention for the bright-red codpiece he wore on stage.

In the 1990s, Cameo's toured, and release the occasional new album, but didn't make much noise on the music charts. In 2000, Cameo quietly released the album "Sexy Sweet Thing" to little fanfare. However, top of the charts or not, each night and to this day, Cameo still mounts the stage with passion and pride for the music that made them revered and respected for so many years.

Larry Blackmon and Cameo are the kind of band that do things their own way. Their strong grooves and funky hooks made their music powerful, sensual, and memorable. Cameo has rocked hard and unashamedly for over 25 years, and their commitment to hot sexy and deliciously funky music makes Cameo Rock 'N Roll Heroes and Funk Legends.

(sources: funkvibe.com, rollingstone.com, theiceberg.com, VH1.com)

CLARENCE CLEMONS

(Born: January 11, 1942, Norfolk, Virginia)

Clarence Clemons was born in Norfolk, Virginia, and is the saxophonist/vocalist who has been a member of Bruce Springsteen's famous E Street Band, since 1973.

Notably, Clarence Clemons has done impressively well as a solo artist also, and scored a duet hit with Jackson Browne, on the smash single "You're a Friend of Mine". But while Clarence professes an impressive solo resume as a saxophonist and singer, he will always be thought of as "The Big Man" of Bruce Springsteen's E Street Band. Clarence Clemons has labored for 30 years alongside Springsteen, creating the masterfully unmistakable saxophone sound on such hits as "Prove It All Night", "Jungleland", "Tenth Avenue Freeze-Out", and "Born to Run".

Clarence Clemons and The E Street Band are an example of how, with talent, hard work, and sheer will power, a blue-collar bar band from New Jersey can become the biggest rock 'n roll group in the world. In the 1980s, Bruce Springsteen, Clarence Clemons and the E Street Band sold out stadiums all over the world in the wake of their multi-platinum album "Born in the U.S.A.", and their mega success continued into the next decade.

In the 1990s, the E Street Band took a temporary break from each other to pursue other projects. The multi-talented Clemons hit the road with his own group, "Clarence Clemons and the Red Bank Rockers". He also performed with Ringo Starr's All- Starr Band and the Jerry Garcia Band. Clarence also did session work with music legends Aretha Franklin, Patti LaBelle, and Roy Orbison.

Talented and versatile, Clarence Clemons created a second career as an actor, playing roles on TV and in film. His TV credits include "The Watcher," "The Human Factor," "The Howie Mandel Show," "The Flash," "Jake and the Fat Man" and "Different Strokes". His film work includes roles in "Fatal Instinct," "The Sentinel," "New York, New York" and "Bill and Ted's Excellent Adventure."

In 2000, the mighty E Street Band reunited with Bruce Springsteen and Clarence Clemons to once again turn the musical world on its ear. The band was rejuvenated and in powerful harmony with their talent and maturity. Their performances were energetic and inspiring.

Clarence Clemons is an amazingly powerful musician. He is The BIG MAN because he has a Big Heart, a Big Soul, and a Big Sexy Rock 'N Roll Sound! Clarence Clemons is a legendary Rock 'N Roll Hero!

(sources: yahoo.com, berkshireweb.com)

RICK JAMES

(Born: February 1, 1948, Buffalo, New York)

James Ambrose Johnson Jr. was born in Buffalo, New York. He was one of eight children, and grew up without a father in the home. But, (Rick) James' mother Mabel Gladden Johnson kept her family together, and gave them support and nurturing.

Young James was the nephew of the Temptations Melvin Franklin, and as (Rick) James grew, he was exposed to a variety of musical styles, including classical, blues, rock, soul and funk. In 1964, (Rick) James enlisted in the Navy Reserve during the Vietnam War. He later regretted his decision and jumped ship, fleeing to Canada.

In Canada, (Rick) James became involved in Toronto's rock scene, hanging out with the likes of later rock legends Neil Young and Joni Mitchell. (Rick) James and Neil Young even formed a group called "Mynah Birds" and went to audition for Smokey Robinson at Motown Records in Detroit. Impressed, Motown signed the group to a record deal, and their debut album was recorded. However, the release of their album was cancelled when Motown found out about (Rick) James' desertion from the US Navy. He had left the Navy to pursue music, but couldn't because he had left the Navy. (Rick) James eventually turned himself in to the FBI and went to prison.

In the 1970s, after his release from prison, and now calling himself "Rick James", he put together a band called "White Cane". Rick wanted to experiment beyond the boundaries of contemporary Black music and mix different musical influences. In 1972, Rick James and White

Cane released the album "The Great White Cane" on MGM Records, however, Rick didn't like the recording because he didn't have control over the production. This would be Rick's only record for MGM, and it would take him over five years to find another record label.

In 1978, Rick James returned to Motown Records and released his solo debut album "Come Get It!", which included the smash hit singles "You and I" and "Mary Jane". Motown gave Rick creative control in the studio, which was traditionally out of character for the notoriously controlling hit factory. It has been suggested that the reason for Rick's production freedom was that Motown's 'Big Money Days' were over, and they were smart enough to see Rick James' earning potential.

In 1979, Rick released his second album "Bustin' Out Of L Seven", and he put together his infamous "Stone City Band", which helped Rick become a cross over rockstar with his ultra heavy "Punk Funk" sound.

In 1980, Rick released the album "Fire It Up", and used a new artist named "Prince" as the tours opening act. However, it's been said that Rick and Prince's personalities clashed, and the conflict hungry media often sensationalized their differences as a sort of musical rivalry or competition.

In 1981, Rick released the hit album, "Street Songs", which produced the mega hit singles, "Super Freak" and "Give It To Me Baby". Rick James was a hit machine during the 1980s. He recorded a new album every year, consistently making the charts with hit single after hit single. He was living the rockstar life style, full of it's inherent trappings of sex, drink, and drugs. However, Rick James' 'Devil may care' rockstar attitude and his increasing sexual and drug addictions got worse and worse. Rick's excessive lifestyle put an awful strain on his body, and he was hospitalized several times in this decadent decade. In 1988, Rick James released the album "Wonderful", which included the number one hit single "Loosey's Rap", but this hit would be Rick's last hit song (not including MC Hammer's use of the Superfreak hook on the rap hit "Can't Touch This").

By the 1990's, Rick James' hard rockin' lifestyle had taken a terrible toll on the talented artist. Rick had become a shadow of his former self, and had slipped into the depths of mind-numbing cocaine and alcohol addiction. But, just as Rick's friends, admirers, and loved ones thought he couldn't sink any lower, in 1991, Rick was arrested and convicted for abusing a woman, holding her against her will, and drugs. Consequently, the legendary Rick James was sent to prison for five long years and forced to deal with all of his physical, psychological, and emotional demons 'Cold-Turkey'.

Admirably, while in prison, Rick James was able kick his drug and alcohol habit, and focus on the one thing that gave him hope, his music. By the time Rick was released from prison in 1996, he had written over 300 new songs, and was ready to mount a musical comeback.

In 1997, 49-year old Rick James, inspired by his love of life, music, and freedom, released his come back album "Urban Rhapsody", and hit the road to promote the album, and show the world the new clean and sober Rick James.

Tragically, Rick's dreams of a successful comeback were delayed. Later that year on tour, Rick suffered a stroke and had to be rushed to the hospital. According to the doctor's reports, Rick's advanced age, history of prolonged substance abuse, and an extremely exhausting stage show, caused a stoke. Rick's stroke affected him physically, and he had to undergo months of physical therapy just to learn how to walk again. But amazingly, Rick not only recovered, but he stormed into the new millennium with a rejuvenated spirit and an outpouring of respect, admiration, and enthusiasm, from longtime fans and the modern generation of entertainers who were weaned on his music and legend.

Shockingly, just when everything seemed to be going his way again, the hammer fell and the final curtain dropped. The mightly Rick James was found dead from heart failure in his Hollywood home on August 6, 2004. He was only 56 years old.

Rick James has had more than his share of ups and downs. However, one thing is certain, Rick James was one hard playing, hard loving, hard rocking son-of-a-gun, and he will always be remembered and respected as a Rock 'N Roll Legend! ("I'm Rick James bitch, goodnight!")

(sources: MTV.com, VH1.com, rollingstone.com, theiceberg.com, funkvibe.com, yahoo.com)

the

'80s

In the 1980s, multi-talented African American Rock acts like Prince, Living Colour, and mega-crossover artists like Hip-Hop supergroup RUN-DMC, toured the world in stadiums and arenas, and delivered the visual and sonic message of professional excellence to thousands of people at a time. Consequently, these highly progressive new-age artists had a strong impact on the social-academic attitude of Black students to achieve their own excellence. Reflectively, during the 1980s, the Black dropout rate declined and African American enrollment in colleges and universities increased. In accordance, and in addition to *The Cosby Show*, the intellectually powerful message of Black Artists became extremely popular.

PRINCE

(Born: June 7, 1958, Minneapolis, Minnesota)

Born Prince Rogers Nelson in Minneapolis, Minnesota, Prince's father, pianist John Nelson, was a member of the Prince Roger Trio, and named his son after the group. As a youth, Prince ran away from the home of his mother and stepfather, and briefly went to live with his father John, who got Prince his first guitar. Later, Prince went to live with the Anderson family, and became very close with young Andre Anderson, who would later adopt the stage name Andre Cymone.

At a young age, Prince was a talented piano and guitar player who wrote and sang his own songs. In junior high school, Prince, Andre, and Andre's cousin Charles, started a cover band called "Grand Central", but by the time they got to high school, Grand Central was renamed "Champagne". In Champagne, Prince began performing his original material for the first time.

In 1976, Prince recorded his first demos, quickly becoming a talented engineer and producer. Prince produced high-quality demos, and from these demos and a massive hype campaign, Prince secured a $100,000 record deal with Warner Bros. Records. At 19 years old, Prince was given total control over the recording and production of his entire project.

After spending twice his allotted budget, in 1978, Prince released his debut album "For You", which featured the single "Soft And Wet", and Prince playing every instrument. Prince had taught himself to play more than 20 instruments, and even though he had spent $200,000 (give or take a few thousand); he amazed everyone at the record label with his versatility and genius.

In 1979, Prince recorded the self-titled album "Prince", which featured the hit singles "Why You Wanna Treat Me So Bad?" and "I Wanna Be Your Lover". Prince also put together a band featuring Dez Dickerson on guitar, Andre Cymone on bass, Matt Fink and Gayle Chapman on keyboards, and Bobby Z on drums.

In 1980, Lisa Coleman replaced Gayle Chapman on the tour to promote the album "Dirty Mind". Interestingly, while opening for Rick James, Prince's androgynous look and sexual lyrics upset Rick, and caused a reported rift between them. After the European leg of their tour was cancelled, Andre Cymone left the band, and was replaced by bassist Brown Mark.

Prince was a prolific songwriter, and wrote enough material for several bands. He wrote an entire album worth of songs for the Minneapolis band "Flyte Time" and they released a self-titled album under their new name "The Time". Prince also created the all-girl group "Vanity 6", for whom he also wrote all the material.

In 1981, Prince released the album "Controversy", and in 1982, he followed with his ground breaking double-album "1999", which featured the hit single "Little Red Corvette". A tour featuring Prince and The Revolution, The Time, and Vanity 6 followed. The end of this tour marked the departure of guitarist Dez Dickerson, and the entry of guitarist Wendy Melvoin.

In 1984, Prince wrote and starred in his own semi-autobiographical movie, the massive hit "Purple Rain". Prince, of course, also wrote all of the music for the film's soundtrack, which featured the mega-hit singles "When Doves Cry", "Let's Go Crazy", "I Would Die 4 U" and "Purple Rain". The album sold over 10 million copies, spent twenty weeks at the top of the album charts, and the world tour was a huge success.

In 1985, Prince wrote and produced the top ten single "Sugar Walls", for Scottish pop sensation Sheena Easton. He also produced an album for sexy singer and percussionist Sheila E., which featured the smash hit

"Erotic City", and later that same year released the psychedelic-inspired album "Around The World in a Day", which featured the hit singles "Raspberry Beret" and "Pop Life".

In 1986, Prince opened his own recording studio and record label called Paisley Park in Minneapolis. He began to work on his second movie, "Under The Cherry Moon", whose number one hit soundtrack album "Parade" featured the smash singles "Kiss" and "Girls and Boys", and "Mountains". In addition, that year Prince wrote the hit single "Manic Monday" for the all-girl rock band "The Bangles", embarked on another spectacular world tour in support of Parade, and promptly disbanded his backing group The Revolution when the tour was finished.

In 1987, Prince formed a new back-up band, keeping keybordist Matt Fink and bassist Brown Mark, and adding Levi Seacer and Mico Weaver on guitar and Sheila E. on drums. Later that year, Prince released the anti-drug album "Sign O' the Times", which featured the hit singles "I Could Never Take The Place of Your Man", "If I Was Your Girlfriend" and "U Got The Look".

Prince's next recording project, The Black Album, was mysteriously recalled before it reached record stores. However, Prince's decision to stop its release made it one of the 1980s' most coveted bootleg albums. Instead, in 1988, Prince released the album "Lovesexy", which featured the hit single "Alphabet Street", and the mega tour that followed included a huge Pink Cadillac that drove around the round stage as sets and lights moved hydrolically into place. Prince literally wore his new band out, going from arena and stadium performances to late night private club gigs in the same evening.

In 1989, Prince produced and recorded the soundtrack album for the year's biggest movie, "Batman" starring Michael Keaton as Batman and Jack Nicholson as the Joker. The Batman soundtrack was a huge commercial smash, topping the US album charts for six weeks. That year Prince also wrote and produced an album for singer Mavis Staples, and in 1990, Irish singer Sinead O'Connor had a number one hit single with Prince's song "Nothing Compares 2 U". Also in 1990,

Prince starred in and produced the soundtrack for the film "Graffiti Bridge", which included the single "Thieves in the Temple".

Prince formed another backing group, the New Power Generation (NPG), for his 1991 hit album "Diamonds And Pearls", which included the hit singles "Cream", "Get Off" and the title track "Diamond and Pearls". In 1992, Prince released the Love Symbol Album which included the hit singles "Money Don't Matter 2 Night", "Sexy MF" and "My Name Is Prince". In 1993, Prince officially changed his name to the unpronounceable symbol ⚥ ; and for many years he was known as "The Artist Formerly Known As Prince". He reportedly did this because of contract disputes with Warner Bros.

In 1994, Prince officially released The Black Album as well as a three CD "Greatest Hits" set. In 1995, Prince released "The Gold Experience", which included the hit singles "Pussy Control", "I Hate You" and "The Most Beautiful Girl In The World", his best-selling single for many years. Also in 1995, Prince appeared at the BRIT Awards in England with the word "slave" written on his face in protest of what he felt was an unfairly long contract with Warner Bros. In 1996, Prince released the album "Chaos & Disorder", which was his last for Warner Bros. Records, and there was no tour.

In late 1996, Prince recorded the three-disc album "Emancipation", released on EMI Records. In 1998, Prince released the four-CD set "Crystal Ball", and in 2000, The Artist Formerly Known As Prince announced that since his Warner Bros. publishing contract expired on New Years Eve 1999, he would formally be re-assuming the name Prince. Remarkably, in 2003, the artist officially and once again known as Prince, recorded, released, and embarked on another sold-out world tour for the timely and successful album Musicology.

Prince is one of the most influential musicians, singer/songwriters, performers and producers in modern rock history. His prolific songwriting prowess is unparalleled, and Prince is without a doubt, a Rock 'N Roll Hero, Legend, and Icon in his own time!

(sources: MTV.com, VH1.com, yahoo.com, rollingstone.com, angelfire.com, theiceberg.com)

TERRENCE TRENT D'ARBY

(Born: March 15, 1962, New York, New York)

T errence Trent D'Arby was born in New York, however it was in Europe that he first made his mark in music. In the early 1980s, Terrence was stationed with the U.S. Army in Germany, where he formed the funk band "Touch". Terrence only released one album with Touch before leaving the group, and eventually moved to London, England, where he secured a deal with CBS Records.

In 1987, Terrence Trent D'Arby's released his solo debut album "Introducing the Hardline According to Terence Trent D'Arby", which included the mega number one hit single "Wishing Well", and the smash hit "Sign Your Name". The album went to number one and sold more than 2,000,000 copies. The tall and sexy 6'1" singer successfully toured in support of his effort, and with impressive videos and performances, won legions of adoring fans.

In 1989, Terrence released the album "Neither Fish Nor Flesh", on which he played most of the instruments, garnishing a much anticipated comparison to Prince, who subscribed to the same school of total control. In 1993, Terrence released the album "Symphony or Damn", and in 1995, he left CBS Records and signed to the Sony/WORK label, releasing the album "Vibrator".

After the Vibrator album, and now long absent from the video channels that made him a international rockstar, Terrence Trent D'Arby toured, and performed modestly in relative obscurity, compared to his former exploits. Many had wondered whatever became of their hero, and could only wait and hope for a come back, or maybe a "Behind The Music" special. The truth is more pleasant and conservative then the traditional, death by drugs, alcohol, sex, or plane crash scenario.

By 2002, Terrence Trent D'Arby had changed his name to Sananda Maitreya (Solar sign Pisces, Chinese Sign Tiger), and quietly released his 5th album "Wild Card" on his own Sananda Records. Now in his forties, Sananda (Terrence) lives a peaceful internationally famous artist's life in Milan, Italy, where he enjoys his fame, money, and music.

Singer/songwriter Terrence Trent D'Arby is a multitalented musician who became internationally famous writing, producing, arranging, and performing his own music. Terrence is remembered by millions of loyal fans, as an amazingly sexy singer, musician, and Rock 'N Roll Hero.

(sources: MTV.com, VH1.com, rollingstone.com, sanandapromotion.com)

TONY MAC ALPINE

(Born: August 29, 1960, USA)

Born in August of 1960, Tony MacAlpine began his study of music as a classically trained pianist and violinist. Tony was considered a musical prodigy, and people wondered what direction such a talented child might take as an adult. Many were astounded when the classically brilliant MacAlpine chose to perform and record as a Heavy Metal guitarist.

In 1986, Tony released the instrumental album "Edge Of Insanity", which combined heavy metal, classical, and elements of jazz-fusion. Tony recorded with bassist Billy Sheehan of the David Lee Roth band and Mr. Big, and drummer Steve Smith of Journey. The album received critical acclaim and Tony amazed listeners with his super-fast guitar work and intellectually vibrant arrangements.

Tony released his next album "Project Driver", which featured himself, vocalist Rob Rock, bassist Rudi Sarzo of Quiet Riot and Ozzy Osborne, and drummer Tommy Aldridge of Ozzy Osborne and Whitesnake. Tony and the band recorded under the name M.A.R.S., but they broke-up soon after the album's release.

In 1987, Tony started his own label Squawk Records, and released the instrumental album "Maximum Security", one of his most popular recordings, showcasing Tony's signature speed along with great feeling and strong melodies. On this record, Tony played all of the guitars, bass, and keyboards, with Atma Anur and Dean Castronovo on drums.

In the 1990s, the prolific virtuoso Tony MacAlpine would record a sting of mind-numbingly brilliant albums, which successfully levitated him to 'Guitar God' status among fans, musicians, and industry magazine enthusiast.

In 1990, now signed to Vertigo Records, Tony released the album "Eyes Of The World", with his new group dubbed "MacAlpine". The band featured Tony on guitar, vocalist Alan Schorn, keyboardist Mark Robertson, and drummer Billy Carmassi. In 1992, now signed to Shrapnel Records, Tony released the instrumental albums "Freedom to Fly", "Madness" in 1993, and "Premonition" in 1994. In 1995, Tony released the album "Evolution", and in 1996 he recorded and released Violent Machine, all the time touring constantly, giving classical piano performances, and appearing at a host of guitar workshops. In 1997, Tony released, "Live Insanity", which is considered his first live CD (excluding bootlegs, and featured his favorite and best loved songs. In 1999, Tony MacAlpine releases the album "Master of Paradise", and in 2001, he released the album "Chromaticity".

The highly progressive heavy metal guitarist Tony MacAlpine is a legend among heavy metal musicians and guitar enthusiast. He has perfected the style of classically influenced rock guitar, and has created a powerfully epic legacy of music in his wake. To all who have come before him, and all who will come after, Tony MacAlpine must be considered a Rock 'N Roll Guitar Hero.

(sources: tonymacalpine.tripod.com, allmusic.com, xtrememusician.com)

JEAN BEAUVOIR

Born in Chicago, Illinois, Jean Beauvoir began playing music as a very young child. By the age of 11, Jean played the guitar, bass and drums. In junior high school Jean was the leader of his own rock band.

When he was still a teenager, the talented young Jean Beauvoir lied about his age and got the job as musical director for Gary US Bonds. This led to gigs with rock 'n roll legends like Chuck Berry and Bo Diddley. During this time Jean became the lead singer for the group "The Flamingos", who had the hit single "I only have eyes for you". Jean accomplished all of this before the age of 15.

At 15-years old, Jean moved to New York, and fell in with the New York City punk rock scene. Jean read in a paper that the punk band "The Plasmatics" were looking for a bass player. After auditioning, Jean was chosen for the band and styled his hair into his signature blond mohawk. The Plasmatics had immediate success, singer Wendy O'Williams and the bands extravagant high-energy stage antics took the world by storm.

However, after three years of constant touring and recording, Jean left The Plasmatics to pursue a solo career. It's been said that Jean turned down job offers from Billy Idol and Prince before excepting the offer of guitarist Little Steven Van Zandt of Bruce Springsteen & the E-Street Band, who convinced Jean to join his new project "Little Steven & Disciple of Soul".

With Little Steven, Jean and the band recorded the albums "Men

Without Women" and "Voice of America". However, after two years of constant recording and touring, Jean left Little Steven's band, and again set out to pursue his long postponed solo career. Frustratingly, despite Jean's experience and musical credentials, every record label he approached turned him down. Eventually, after securing good management and auditioning off his mohawk, Jean Beauvoir finally signed to Virgin Records, UK, and began recording his first solo album.

Jean Beauvoir's first single "Feel the Heat", was chosen by Sylvester Stallone for his hit film "COBRA". From this exposure, Jean signed a US record deal with CBS/Columbia Records, and sold over a million copies of his album "Drums along the Mohawk". Jean's reputation as a songwriter and producer spread and he would work with internationally famous groups and artists like The Ramones, Deborah Harry, Lionel Richie, Nile Rogers, Nona Hendrix, Desmond Child, and KISS.

Between production gigs, Jean recorded the album "Jacknifed", and toured with the Eurythmics, and Tina Turner. Jean Beauvoir's next album was "The Awakening Part 1", and Jean continued his work in movie soundtracks with songs for Stephen King's hit film "Pet Semetary" and Wes Craven's thriller "Shocker".

Jean signed a reported million-dollar deal with Los Angeles' Interscope Records and formed his band "Crown of Thorns". However, the highly anticipated album was shelved due to a long recording process and changing tides in the record industry. But offers from labels in Europe and Japan to distribute the album finally got it released over seas, and the band set out on tour in support of the album. Jean Beauvoir and Crown of Thorns triumphantly toured with headlining mega bands like Bon Jovi and Van Halen.

Since 1993, Jean Beauvoir and Crown of Thorns have recorded and released 5 albums overseas, which are available in the US as imports. In 1996, Virgin Records released a best of Jean Beauvoir album entitled "Rockin in The Streets", and in 2000, Jean cut off his signature mohawk and released the album "Destiny Unknown" with

Crown of Thorns, on Voodoo Island Records.

In 2001, Jean released an acoustic solo album, which featured new material and new versions of his favorite songs from the past, and in 2002, Jean Beauvoir and Crown of Thorns released their 6th album "KARMA", which featured 11 new tracks, and a duet with German singer DORO.

Jean Beauvoir is a highly respected singer/songwriter, musician, producer and performer who has dedicated over 30 years to cutting edge rock 'n roll, and has earned the respect and adoration of his fans, colleagues, and peers, making him a first class Rock 'N Roll Hero!

(sources: jeanbeauvoir.com, jeanbeauvoir-tribute.com, rollingstone.com, VH1.com)

DOUG PINNICK (KING'S X)

(Born: September 3, 1950, Braidwood, Illinois)

Doug Pinnick grew up in a musical family in Braidwood, Illinois, where his first instrument was the Baritone Saxophone. When Doug was 14, his family moved to Joliet, Illinois. Doug sang with several local bands, picking up the bass guitar at the age of 22. During the 1970's, Doug gigged locally for several more years with bands like "Servant" and the "Doug Pinnick Band".

While playing bass for the "Carl Henshaw Band", Doug met future King's X drummer Jerry Gaskill, and in 1980, while both were touring with the Christian rock band "Petra", Doug and Jerry met future King's X guitarist Ty Tabor. The new band was initially called "The Edge", and specialized in top 40 covers. The Edge played the Missouri bar and club scene for a few years, and in 1983, changed their name to "Sneak Preview", releasing a self-titled album with original material.

In 1985, the band was promised a record deal in Texas, and moved to Houston. However, the deal fell through, but the band met Z.Z. Top's video producer Sam Taylor, who suggested the name "King's X". Intrepidly, after a couple of years of performing and promoting themselves in Texas, King's X eventually signed a deal with the heavy metal label Megaforce Records.

In 1988, Doug and King's X released their debut album "Out of the Silent Planet", which was powerfully driven by a melodic and spiritual theme. In 1989, King's X released their second album, the now legendary "Gretchen Goes to Nebraska", which included the hit single and MTV video "Over My Head". Many of their fans consider the album a classic, and feel this effort really put Doug and the band on the map.

In 1990, King's X released their third album "Faith Hope Love", which was their first album to reach the top 100, and included the hit single "It's Love". The success of this third album led to a major-label deal with Atlantic Records, and the band toured extensively in the US and Europe. In 1992, King's X released their self-titled fourth album "King's X", on Atlantic Records, and in 1994, King's X released their fifth album "Dogman", which included the ultra heavy title-track single and video "Dogman". King's X embarked on a world tour in support of Dogman, and made a memorable appearance at the Woodstock '94 festival. In 1996, Doug and King's X released their sixth album "Ear Candy", and in 1997, King's X released the band's 'best of album', which included a live version of "Over My Head" from the Woodstock '94 festival.

For almost 20 years, Doug Pinnick had performed and recorded almost exclusively with King's X, but in 1998, Doug released his solo album "Poundhound: Massive Grooves...", which Doug recorded at his own studio "The Hound Pound". That same year, Doug and King's X signed with Metal Blade Records and released their seventh studio album "Tapehead", which King's X produced themselves.

In 2000, King's X released their eighth studio album "Please Come Home... Mr. Bulbous", and in 2001, Doug released his second solo album "Pineapple Skunk", and toured the US with his solo band "Poundhound". Later that same year, King's X released their ninth studio album "Manic Moonlight".

Doug Pinnick is a powerful example of a talented, driven, and independent soul, who with his band King's X, has taken all challenges, and risen to a level of musical excellence that few musicians ever achieve. For his brilliance, perseverance and class, Doug Pinnick is justly considered a Rock 'N Roll Hero!

(sources: yahoo.com, rollingstone.com, VH1.com, MTV.com, kingsx.net)

FISHBONE

Fishbone was formed in 1978, by drummer "Fish" Fisher, bassist Jon Norwood Fisher, guitarist Kendall Jones, vocalist, keyboards, and trombone player Chris Dowd, trumpet player Walt Kibby, and vocalist and saxophonist Angelo Moore. Early on the band favored a multitude of musical tastes and styles, including punk, funk, jazz and most of all ska. After years of toiling in the Los Angeles club scene, in 1985, Fishbone released their self-titled mini album "Fishbone", which showcased their signature ska rhythms, and strong guitar work, mixed with punk-like speed and energy.

In 1986, Fishbone released the album "In Your Face", which got them critical attention and respect in both the growing ska/hardcore and hard rock/heavy metal scene. In 1988, Fishbone released the album "Truth & Soul", which included the single "Bonin' in the Boneyard" and a hip remake of the Curtis Mayfield classic, "Freddie's Dead". This album had a strong political message and included amazing vocal performances by the entire band. It has been said that one of Fishbone's greatest musical strengths is their ability to share vocals and add powerful R&B-like harmonies to their heavy arrangements. After "Truth & Soul" Fishbone added guitarist John Bigham, formerly with Miles Davis, and in 1989, released the album "The Reality of My Surroundings", which is their best selling album to date, and garnished them MTV video airplay, bringing the mighty Fishbone into the mainstream.

Fishbone released the critically acclaimed album "Give A Monkey A Brain and He'll Swear He's the Center of the Universe", which included the super heavy single and video "Swim". In the wake of the notorious police beating of Rodney King, and in the fire and smoke darkened shadow of race riots and civil unrest, Fishbone released the album "The Warmth of Your Breath", and toured extensively, including a memorable performance at the England's Reading Festival in 1993.

Eventfully, that same year guitarist Kendall Jones left the band for personal reasons. Reportedly thinking that Kendall was the victim of religious brainwashing, bassist John Norwood Fisher, attempted to "rescue" Kendall and return him to Los Angeles. Consequently, a lawsuit involving the use of the term 'Kidnapping' was brought against Fisher by Kendall's family. Fishbone continued to tour, but soon after the Kendall Jones incident, keyboardist and vocalist Chris Dowd was mysteriously ejected from the band.

After this, Fishbone left their longtime record label Columbia Records, and signed to Rowdy/Arista Records, and released the album "Chim-Chim's Badass Revenge". Unfortunately, Arista discontinued their subsidiary label Rowdy Records, which left Fishbone without a record deal. As a result, guitarist Jon Bigham left the band, and founding member "Fish" Fisher, decided that Fishbone couldn't pay his bills, and he also left the group.

Regardless of their label affiliation, when it comes to American rock bands, it would be difficult to top Fishbone's musical credentials. Their powerfully relentless sound and energy pushed the boundaries of rock, ska, R&B and hard-core. Along with founding the west coast chapter of the Black Rock Coalition, for over 20 years, Fishbone have been champions of racial equality in music; and for this, Fishbone are justly revered as Rock 'N Roll Heroes!

(sources: members.tripod.com, rollingstone.com, theiceberg.com,, MTV.com, VH1.com, yahoo.com)

LIVING COLOUR

Living Colour was originally formed in 1984 as a trio, by guitarist Vernon Reid of London, England, a founder of New York's Black Rock Coalition, bassist Muzz Skillings and drummer William Calhoun of New York. Vernon had come to New York at the age of two, and studied performing arts at Manhattan Community College. Both Muzz and Will were also accomplished musicians who had studied at New York City College and Berkley College of Music in Boston, respectively.

Living Colour's classic lineup was completed by the addition of vocalist Corey Glover of New York, who had just completed an acting role in Oliver Stone's award winning film "Platoon". Vernon had heard Corey singing happy birthday at a mutual friend's birthday party, and thought Corey would be a perfect fit for the group.

Living Colour started playing the New York club scene in 1986, and became popular playing four times a month at the world famous punk rock club CBGB's. The buzz about the band's energetic and powerful live shows grew fast, and Rolling Stones' frontman Mick Jagger came to CBGB's to hear them. It's been said that Mick was so impressed with Living Colour that he produced two demos for them, and the hype and attention from that collaboration help them score a deal with Epic Records.

In 1988, Living Colour released their debut album "Vivid", which included the Grammy award winning hit single and video "Cult Of

Personality". MTV played the video constantly, and Vivid earned Living Colour worldwide acclaim, rising to number six on the US charts. They band toured tirelessly in support of Vivid, and even joined the Rolling Stones on their Steel Wheels stadium tour.

In 1990, Living Colour released their second album "Time's Up", which won them another Grammy Award, and included the controversial single 'Elvis Is Dead' featuring Rock Legend Little Richard. In 1991, the band performed on the first Lollapalooza tour, and released the EP "Biscuits". Following the release of Biscuits, bassist Muzz Skillings quit the band and became a Firefighter. Bassist Doug Wimbish of Connecticut was called to fill in on upcoming tour dates, and soon after the band offered Doug a permanent job, as they continued their grueling touring and performing schedule.

In 1993, Living Colour released their third full-length album "Stain", which included the single "Love Rears its Ugly Head", and the band again toured non-stop in 1993. In 1994, they released a cover of Cream's "Sunshine Of your Love", for the soundtrack of the Arnold Schwarzenegger film "True Lies". Also in 1994, The band signed a deal with Sony Records and entered the recording studio in London, to begin work on a their fourth full-length album.

However, just three months later, in early 1995, Vernon Reid announced the break up of the band, saying he found more creative satisfaction in his solo projects. A sort of 'greatest hits' album called "Pride" was released in November 1995, featuring four previously unreleased tracks from the 1994 studio sessions.

After five long years of solo projects from each member, In 2000, the band that is Living Colour reunited on stage at CBGB's, the place where it all began some fourteen years earlier. The club was packed beyond capacity with loyal fans, eager journalist, and die-hard supporters who had dreamed of the day when this magical band might find their way back together.

The re-united Living Colour toured the US and Europe in triumph, acclaim and overwhelming support from audiences worldwide.

In 2002, the band entered the recording studio in Boston and to begin work on a new album entitled "Kaleidoscope", released in 2003.

The all-Black rock band Living Colour comprised of guitarist Vernon Reid, drummer William Calhoun, singer Corey Glover, bassist Muzz Skillings, and later bassist Doug Wimbish, set the standard for successful Black rock bands in the late 1980s and 1990s. Living Colour's highly energetic and political brand of rock, punctuated by Vernon Reid's lightning-fast guitar work and Corey Glover's amazing voice, earned the band multiple awards, and international acclaim from fans and critics alike. Living Colour stand proudly as an example of how an ethnically expressive band can overcome the inherent barriers of industrial, institutional and social racism to become world renowned Rock 'N Roll Heroes.

(sources: VH1.com, MTV.com, livedaily.citysearch.com, rollingstone.com, livingcolour.net)

24-7 SPYZ

T he all-Black hard rock band 24-7 SPYZ was formed in the Bronx, New York, in 1988 by singer Peter "Fluid" Forest, guitarist Jimi Hazel, bassist Rick Skatore, and drummer Anthony Johnson. The SPYZ drew from rock, metal, funk, punk, rap and reggae influences to create a unique, energetic and powerful sound that quickly won critical acclaim.

In 1989, 24-7 SPYZ released their debut album "Harder Than You", which featured the singles "Grandma Dynamite", "Ballots Not Bullets", "Tango Skin Polka" and a powerful re-make of Kool & The Gang's hit song "Jungle Boogie". The SPYZ toured relentlessly in support of their debut release, and gained legions of loyal fans on the road. In late 1989, the band was due to perform a concert in Berkeley, California the night after the big 1989 'Loma Prieta' earthquake. Admirably, instead of canceling the gig completely, the SPYZ performed a free impromptu concert at a local frat-house, astounding and amazing the frenzied college crowd, and raising the spirits of a city grieving in the wake of an enormous natural disaster.

In 1990, 24-7 SPYZ released their second album "Gumbo Millennium", which included the singles "Racism", "Don't Push Me" and the environmentally conscious "Valdez 27 Million". Following the release of Gumbo Millennium, vocalist Peter Fluid and drummer Anthony Johnson left the group, and were replaced by vocalist Jeff Brodnax and drummer Joel Maitoza.

In 1991, the new line-up of 24-7 SPYZ released the album "This Is 24-7 Spyz", and in 1992, they released the album "Strength in Numbers". The SPYZ released their next two albums, "Temporarily Disconnected" in 1994 and "6" in 1995, which was distributed overseas on the European label Enemy Records. In 1996, with new drummer Carlton Smith in tow, the band released the material from the album '6' in the US, under the new album title "Heavy Metal Soul By the Pound", distributed by a Colorado based indy record label.

In the years approaching 2000, 24-7 SPYZ have toured and quietly released quality material. However, it is the original line-up of Fluid, Hazel, Skatore, and Johnson, that will always be remembered for the excitement, power, and brilliance, that made 24-7 SPYZ Rock 'N Roll Heroes.

(sources: rollingstone.com, allmusic.com)

BAD BRAINS

Formed in Washington DC, in 1978, by guitarist Gary "Dr. Know" Miller, bassist Darryl Jennifer, and brothers Joseph "HR" Hudson on vocals and Earl Hudson on drums. Bad Brains started out playing seventies jazz/rock fusion, but later began introducing a mixture of reggae and punk into their live shows. Consequently, the band became pioneers of punk's hardcore fringe, influencing nearly every subsequent hardcore outfit to come after them. As an all-Black rock band, they were an inspiration to bands like Living Colour and the now famous Black Rock Coalition.

In 1980, Bad Brains released their recording "ëOmega Sessions", which was the band's first multi-track recording session, and introduced Bad Brains to the hardcore/punk scene in Washington DC. To this day, the Bad Brains' single "Pay to Cum" remains a hardcore classic, but much of the band's early music was never well recorded. The single "Pay to Cum " was available only in its rare 45rpm form, and on the band's self-titled cassette.

In 1983, Bad Brains released the album "Rock for Light", produced by "Cars" guitarist Ric Ocasek, which had one side of reggae and one side of hardcore. Bad Brains is famous for their intense political and masculine personas. Reflectively, singer HR is historically quick-tempered, and during a show in Kansas, HR reportedly split open the skull of a local skinhead with the microphone stand, sending him to the hospital. Likewise, on the Beastie Boys tour in Montreal, Canada,

HR again reportedly attacked the Beastie's manager and sent him to a local emergency room.

Despite their explosive exploits, in 1988, Bad Brains released their long awaited hit album "I Against I", which was heralded as an all rock and hardcore masterpiece, and included the perennial hit single "Re-ignition". But this recording and subsequent tour left the band fragmented, with HR and Earl Hudson wanting to do more reggae, and Dr. Know and Darryl Jennifer wanting to record and perform more rock. As a result of the rift, the brothers Hudson left Bad Brains in 1989, and the two recorded reggae albums under HR's name. The remaining Bad Brains members recruited Trinidad-born vocalist Israel Joseph-I to replace HR and recorded and released the album "Rise".

After years of touring and performing independently of each other, in 1995, HR and Earl Hudson returned to Bad Brains, and the re-united band released the album "God of Love". In the years approaching the new millennium, Bad Brains have collectively and individually continued making their marks in popular music and hardcore through their recording, producing, and collaborating within the international music scene. Bad Brains shattered musical, cultural and racial barriers with their radically contrasting forays into dub, reggae, rock and punk. Their lofty convictions and 'Positive Mental Attitude' (PMA) are the overriding philosophies of Bad Brains, who have always been unafraid to stand up against wrongs that need to be righted. Over the past 25 years, Bad Brains have successfully gotten away with their overtly Rastafarian political views, over the top antics, and have become hard-core Icons, and Rock 'N Roll Heroes.

(sources: hitsquick.com, thegauntlet.com, rolling stone.com)

RUN DMC

The pioneering New York based rap group responsible for the mainstreaming of Rap and Hip Hop, and it's crossover and mixture in rock 'n roll, was formed by the brother of music producer Russell Simmons, Joseph "RUN" Simmons, Darryl "DMC" McDaniels, and Jason "Jam Master Jay" Mizell. The group originally called themselves "Orange Crush" in the early 1980s, but became RUN-DMC in 1982.

They had known each other as children in the Hollis, Queens, district of New York City, and after hype was generated from their demos, RUN-DMC and Jam Master Jay signed to Profile Records for an advance of $2,500, and scored a hit with the single "It's Like That". The B-side of their single "Sucker M.C.'s", also garnished a lot of attention, and with no instruments apart from a drum machine and scratching from a turntable, RUN-DMC with their B-boy style street clothing, and tennis shoes, proceeded to change the world. In 1984, in the wake of their single success, their debut album was the first in Hip-Hop to earn gold status. They furiously toured, and appeared in the 1980s era movie "Krush Groove", a fictional account of the life of RUN's brother and future music mogul Russell Simmons, who then was co-founder of Def Jam Records with now legendary producer Rick Rubin.

In 1986, RUN-DMC released their landmark super-hit album "Raising Hell", which included the hit singles "Rock Box", "King

Of Rock", "My Adidas", and the international crossover mega single responsible for bringing Hip-Hop into the mainstream, "Walk This Way". The hit single featured guest performances by Steve Tyler and Joe Perry of Aerosmith, and was a re-make of their 1970s hit of the same name. Its internationally popular performance video, featuring Tyler, Perry and RUN-DMC, helped rocket the single into the US charts top five. The single also effectively rejuvenated the long waning career of Aerosmith, and sent the legendary '70s rockers soaring again into future rock 'n roll success and monumental wealth and acclaim in the MTV era.

By 1987, Raising Hell had sold three million copies in the US, becoming the first Hip-Hop album to hit number one on the R&B charts, the first to hit the top ten on the pop album charts, and the first to go platinum. RUN-DMC also became the first Hip-Hip group to have a video on MTV, the first on the cover of Rolling Stone magazine, and the first non-athletes to get an endorsement deal with the Adidas sporting company. In the thrust of their superstardom, RUN-DMC headlined arena tours around the world, appeared on TV constantly, and even making their own big-screen movie, "Tougher Than Leather".

However, in the 1990s, with the insurgence of more political and cutting edge Hip-Hop acts like Public Enemy, NWA, and many others who achieved success on the coattails of the mighty RUN-DMC, the trailblazing group found their own popularity waning and their style of rapping becoming 'outdated'. Subsequently, in the shadow of substance abuse and legal woes, Run and DMC experienced religious conversions, and after the release of 1993s religiously inspired album "Down With The King", RUN-DMC faded quietly into the background of an increasingly edgier 1990s Hip-Hop scene marred by violence, murder, assassination, and controversy.

In 2000, RUN-DMC and Jam Master Jay would experience renewed popularity from the modern music scene, generated by a popular "Behind the Music" documentary and contemporary respect for their pioneering work in the 1980s. As a result, in 2001, RUN-DMC released the star-studded come back album "Crown Royal", and after years of inactivity, returned to the road, and into the hearts of a new generation of old-school fans, touring with good friends Aerosmith and hit sensation Kid Rock.

Tragically, their come-back glory would be short lived. On October 30, 2002, the legendary DJ Jam Master Jay of RUN-DMC was shot to death in a Queens recording studio. RUN-DMC was scheduled to perform during half-time at the Washington Wizards basketball game the next day, but that performance never happened. Jam Master Jay was a unique individual, and the very embodiment of Hip-Hop.

RUN-DMC played the game, and came up winners. They broke trail, and pioneered the way to a land of sweet milk and golden honeys for the multitudes of popular Hip-Hop artist who would follow their lead to stardom. RUN-DMC were called the "Beatles of Hip Hop" by Public Enemy's Chuck-D. They were Great! RUN-DMC and Jam Master Jay, are Rock 'N Roll Legends and Rap/Hip-Hop Icons.

(sources: MTV.com, VH1.com, rollingstone.com, theiceberg.com, 411mania.com)

the

'90s

In the 1990s, African American Rockers led the way toward more cultural acceptance and diversity in rock music. Racially diverse (African American & Caucasian) artists like Lenny Kravitz, Ben Harper, and Alana Davis were celebrated examples of increased multicultural and cross-cultural acceptance in American society.

Also, the 1990s brought with it a profound sexual revolution in rock music. Led by the multi-platinum and multi-award winning talents of African American female artists like Janet Jackson, Tracy Chapman, and Lauryn Hill, the 1990's became the decade which more than ever before, established women as a powerful presence in mainstream rock music.

JANET JACKSON

(Born: May 16, 1966, Gary, Indiana)

J anet Damita Jo Jackson was the youngest of the nine children born into the musical Jackson family of Gary, Indiana. Janet's brothers were the famous 1970s pop group The Jackson 5 (featuring Michael Jackson) and Janet began occasionally performing with her brothers when she was a young child. But, as a youth, Janet was more interested in her acting, than her signing.

As a child and teenager, Janet Jackson appeared on the TV shows Good Times, Diff'rent Strokes and Fame. When she was 16, her father, family manager and patriarch Joseph Jackson, encouraged Janet to follow in her brothers' footsteps and consider singing professionally. In 1982, Janet signed to A&M Records and released her debut self-titled album "Janet Jackson", which she followed up with the album "Dreamstreet" in 1984.

In 1986, Janet released her landmark album "Control", which included the smash hit title track "Control", the sexually confident hit single "What Have You Done For Me Lately?", and the flirtatious "When I Think Of You". Flying from Los Angles to Minneapolis, Janet recorded the hit album with now legendary producers Jimmy Jam and Terry Lewis. Music videos also played a large part in Janet's success. With angelic features and an award winning smile, Janet and videos were the perfect match.

In 1989, Janet released another hit album "Rhythm Nation 1814", which included the smash title track "Rhythm Nation", the vibrant

"Miss You Much", the hard rocking "Black Cat", and the sultry "Love Will Never Do". All of which garnished dazzlingly popular videos on MTV, and many other international video channels. On the heels of the hit album and videos, Janet embarked on her first tour as an adult artist. Due to Janet's huge worldwide popularity, her first tour was as a headliner. The Rhythm Nation World Tour 1990 gave fans the chance to see the adult Janet perform live for the very first time. The tour was lavish, exciting, and exhausting for the youngest Jackson.

In 1991, Janet signed a multi-million dollar mega deal with Virgin Records, and that same year she starred in the film "Poetic Justice" with Tupac Shakur. In 1993, Janet released another self-titled album simply called "Janet", which produced six hit singles including "That's The Way Love Goes" and "If". All of the subsequent videos featured a much sexier Janet, expressing almost erotic sensuality.

In 1995, Janet Jackson teamed up for a duet with her mega star brother Michael Jackson on the single "Scream", which earned them both a Grammy Award, and also dawned the futuristic eight million dollar video. The very next year, in 1996, Janet released a greatest hits-like album called "Design of a Decade", which included the best of her stellar singles and performances.

Over the next five years, Janet would continue to dominate the popular music scene with mind-blowingly beautiful videos, ultra sexy and extravagant tours and wonderful performances. So it came as no surprise that, in 2001, Janet Jackson would be honored at the inaugural MTV Icon award show, as one of the most influential artists in contemporary pop, rock and R&B music. Also, that same year, Janet released her next hit album "All For You", in April. However, most notably in 2004, Janet exposed her bare breast (tiddy) to a potential billion people on a world-wide televised Superbowl half-time performance. The outcry and controversy was so enormous, that it took the nation's mind off of Michael's kiddy problems, Institutional Racism, and The War in Iraq, for almost a month! Janet Jackson rules the universe.

The beautiful and ultra talented Janet Jackson is one of the most successful female performers in the last 30 years. Her world-wide career sales total almost 60 million records sold, and she is still going strong. Janet's parents taught her and her siblings to never give up, and her drive, ambition, talent, and beauty, have propelled the youngest of Joseph and Katherine Jackson's children to the level of Mega star and Rock 'N Roll Icon.

(sources: rollingstone.com, MTV.com, VH1.com, janet-jackson.com, kidzworld.com)

LENNY KRAVITZ

(Born: May 26, 1964, Brooklyn, New York)

Lenny Kravitz was born in Brooklyn, New York, the only child of TV news producer Sy Kravitz and African American actress Roxie Roker, best known for her part as Helen Willis on the '70s hit TV show "The Jeffersons".

In 1974, Lenny and his family moved to Los Angeles where his mother was working in television, and young Lenny won a spot in the famed California Boys Choir. As a teenager Lenny, continued singing, was involved in acting, and developed the flamboyant new-age rockstar persona "Romeo Blue".

After high school, Lenny began playing music seriously, and performed all over the Los Angeles area, recording demos, and seeking a record deal. Success did not come quickly. While performing as Romeo Blue, Lenny met Cosby Show actress Lisa Bonet. The two began living together, and eventually went to Las Vegas in 1987 to get married. A year later in 1988, Lenny and Lisa's daughter Zoe was born.

In 1989, dawning his signature locks, Lenny Kravitz recorded and released his debut album "Let Love Rule", which included a single of the same name, and a video directed by wife Lisa. Sadly, in 1991, just as Lenny was gaining respect and popularity in the music business, he and wife Lisa Bonet, separated. Later 1991, Lenny released his second album "Mama Said", which included the single "Always On The Run", and "It Ain't Over 'Til It's Over", showing a more serious, pain-ridden man, in great anguish over his failing marriage.

In 1993, Lenny's divorce from Lisa Bonet became final, and he released his mega hit album "Are You Gonna Go My Way". The title track earned Lenny a MTV Video Award for Best Male Video, and two Grammy nominations for Best Rock Song and Best Rock Vocal Performance. Lenny also toured extensively in support of the album and video, and blossomed into a dynamic entertainer.

During the recording of Lenny's fourth album "Circus", released in 1995, Lenny learned that his mother, actress Roxie Roker, was terminally ill and dying. Consequently, the album "Circus" has a definingly darker and apocalyptic tone to it, garnishing the edgy single and video "Rock and Roll is Dead".

In 1998, Lenny, having cut off his signature locks, released his fifth album '5', which included the hit single and video "Fly Away", and won him the 1999 Grammy award for Best Male Rock Vocal Performance, making him the first African American to win a Grammy in a rock category.

In 2000, Lenny's re-make of the Guess Who's "American Woman" won him the Best Male Rock Vocal Performance Grammy again, and he released a Greatest Hits CD, which included 14 of his biggest singles, plus the new hit single and video "Again". In 2002, Lenny Kravitz released his self-titled 6th album "Lenny", which included a hit single and video "Dig in". He appeared on several TV shows, including a live concert movie on cable music channel VH1, and continues to forage on into the new millennium, recreating his look, style and music at will, collecting millions of loyal fans as he goes.

Lenny Kravitz is a multi-talented instrumentalist, singer, songwriter, producer, and performer, who has lived his life and pursued his career according to his own set of unwavering personal beliefs and undying perseverance. Lenny has done it his way, and has reaped what he has sown. For his success, accomplishments, and the adoration of millions, Lenny Kravitz has risen to the pantheon of Rock 'N Roll Hero and Superstar!

(sources: MTV.com, VH1.com, rollingstone.com, theiceberg.com, lennykravitz.net)

TRACY CHAPMAN

(Born: March 30, 1964, Cleveland, Ohio)

Born in Cleveland, Ohio, and raised in a working class neighborhood, Tracy Chapman learned how to play guitar as a child, and by her teens, began to write her own songs. The daughter of estranged parents, following high school, Tracy attended college on a scholarship and studied anthropology and African studies. While in college, Tracy became interested in the folk/rock and the singer/songwriter scene, and began performing at coffee houses. She became well known in the campus folk club, and eventually recorded a set of demos at the college radio station. Another student at her college, Brian Koppelman, loved Tracy's music and recommended her to his father, Charles Koppelman, who ran SBK Publishing.

In 1986, Tracy signed a deal with SBK Publishing and a management contract with Elliot Roberts, who had worked with Neil Young and Joni Mitchell. In 1987, Tracy signed to Elektra Records and released her debut album in the spring of 1988. She went on tour supporting the band 10,000 Maniacs, and within a few months, she was invited to play at the internationally televised concert for Nelson Mandela's 70th Birthday Party at Wembley Stadium in London. It was at this performance, where during the satellite-linked concert, Tracy got her big break. When the scheduled headliner dropped out, Tracy's slot was extended and her performance received thunderous applause, winning the hearts of the audience and the millions watching worldwide.

Soon after, her single "Fast Car" entered the top ten on the singles charts, and by the end of the year her album had gone multi-platinum. The next year, in 1989, Tracy Chapman won the Grammy Award for Best New Artist. After her stunning debut, Tracy performed with Peter Gabriel, Sting and U2 on a worldwide tour in aid of Amnesty International. Unfortunately, afterwards she lost momentum, and though her second album "Crossroads" was number one in the UK, and in the top ten in the US, her title track single "Crossroads" was only a minor hit.

After this, Tracy took sometime to herself away from the spotlight, but her next album "Matters Of The Heart", in 1992, suffered as a result of Tracy's long absence from the music scene, and even failed to make the US Top 50 album chart. In 1995, after another three year hiatus, Tracy released her album "New Beginning", which included the hit single "Give Me One Reason". This album found a much wider audience, and catapulted Tracy Chapman back into the international spotlight.

Triumphantly, in 2000, Tracy's next album "Telling Stories", which dawned the title track single "Telling Stories" and "It's OK", was considered by many her best work since her debut album.

Tracy Chapman's auspiciously successful career will forever be remembered for the timelessly personalized songs that she shared and sang with an internationally grateful audience. Her legions of loyal fans have forever secured her cult status, and permanently assured her legacy as a Rock 'N Roll Hero.

(sources: rollingstone.com, allmusic.com, theiceberg.com, VH1.com)

ICE-T (BODY COUNT)

(Born: February 16, 1958, Newark, New Jersey)

Born Tracy Marrow in Newark, New Jersey, young Tracy (Ice-T) later moved to California, and grew up in rough South Central Los Angeles. While in LA, Tracy (Ice-T) began rapping as a teenager and adopted his now-infamous persona "Ice-T", reportedly inspired by the pimp and writer Iceberg Slim.

After high school, Ice joined the army. Upon his return to Los Angeles, Ice-T recorded several rap singles and appeared in the Hip-Hop films "Rappin'" and "Breakin'". In 1987, Ice-T signed a record deal with Sire/Warner Bros. Records and released his major-label debut "Rhyme Pays". The album quickly went gold, selling over 500,000 copies.

In 1988, Ice-T released his second album "Power", which also went gold, winning Ice-T critical acclaim for his rhyming and lyrics. That year, Ice recorded the title soundtrack single for the mega hit movie "Colors", starring Sean Penn and Robert Duvall. In 1989, Ice-T took on the fight against music censorship and released his book "The Iceberg / Freedom of Speech... Just Watch What You Say", which garnished Ice much deserved praise for this highly political effort.

In 1991, now an internationally known Hip-Hop superstar, Ice-T returned to films with a starring role in the critically acclaimed and wildly popular "New Jack City", and also that year, Ice-T released another successful album "O.G.: Original Gangster".

Everything seemed to be going great for Ice; however, his next musical project would prove to be his most arduous. In 1992, Ice-T's next recording project was the now infamous heavy metal/hardcore band "Body Count", which achieved worldwide attention for the inclusion of the track "Cop Killer" and singles like "KKK Bitch", "Bowels Of The Devil" and "Momma's Gotta Die Tonight".

Body Count had performed the year before during the first Lollapalooza music festival tour in 1991, with Ice on Vocals, Ernie-C on lead guitar, guitarist D-Roc, bassist Mooseman and drummer Beatmaster V, whom Ice knew from Crenshaw High School in South Central Los Angeles. Although shrouded in controversy, Body Count's material contained a positive anti-racism/anti-drug message, addressing institutionalized racism, bigotry and genocide. The band played the opening slot on the Guns N' Roses/Metallica North American stadium tour, and their album eventually sold over 800,000 copies.

However, the Los Angeles Police Department took extreme exception to the song "Cop Killer", and viewed it as dangerous and inflammatory. A fury of negative publicity was aimed at Ice-T by the law enforcement community, and he even became number two on the FBI National Threat list. Even acclaimed actor Charlton Heston, then the head of the National Riflemen Association (NRA), verbally attacked Ice-T, reading out the lyrics to "KKK Bitch" to shocked shareholders at Time Warner's annual meeting. Other opponents of Ice-T and Body Count were George H. Bush, Oliver North, and the Texas Policeman's Association, who called for a nationwide boycott of Time Warner, including Disneyland, which threatened to cost millions of dollars. However, when Ice-T and the record company employees began receiving death threats, Ice himself made the decision to replaced the track on the album with a spoken word message from former Dead Kennedy's frontman and anti-censorship activist Jello Biafra. Ironically, the single "Cop Killer" appeared in the Warner Bros. blockbuster movie "Batman Returns", popular with kids, adults and families everywhere.

Even though Warner Bros. outwardly supported Ice-T as their artist, the controversy was secretly souring Ice-T's relationship with the record company. Ice-T and Body Count left Warner Bros., and signed with Virgin Records. In 1993, Ice recorded a second Body Count album "Born Dead", which didn't attract any controversy at all. Ice-T became increasingly visible publicly, speaking out on college campuses and in the media against censorship and even writing another book about this experience.

Since then, Ice-T has become a much respected multi-media, TV, and movie star, in addition to his musical accomplishments. Ice has appeared in a number of movies and television shows, including the movies Trespass, Surviving the Game, 3000 Miles to Graceland, and the TV series "Players", "New York Undercover", and the very popular "Law & Order" series.

Ice-T has made an indelible mark in modern culture. His uncompromising style of expression has spawned millions of record sales and adoring fans worldwide. Ice-T is the kind of artist that rides the edge and often crosses the line, making him a rebel, a maverick, and a modern day Rock 'N Roll Hero!

(sources: rollingstone.com, theiceberg.com, VH1.com)

DARIUS RUCKER
(HOOTIE & THE BLOWFISH)

(Born May 13, 1966, Charleston, SC)

Born and raised in Charleston, South Carolina, Darius Rucker grew up on the sounds of Motown. Darius spent his childhood days in Charleston playing broomstick guitar, performing in front of imaginary audiences, and dreaming of becoming a famous singer. As Darius grew older he replaced the broom, and learned how to play an actual guitar, becoming a skillful songwriter, and soulful singer.

In 1986, while attending the University of South Carolina, Darius met guitarist Mark Bryan and bassist Dean Felber. Along with a drummer, they began performing at the college, and around the local area, building a following, and sharpening their musical skills.

In 1989, Darius and the band, now sporting the memorable moniker of "Hootie & the Blowfish", acquired drummer and songwriter Jim "Soni" Sonefeld, and with this classic line-up in place, really began to make some serious noise in the southeast region of the country. Packing concert halls, and selling there own recordings, Hootie & the Blowfish attracted the attention of several major record labels.

In 1994, Hootie & the Blowfish released their major label debut album "Cracked Rear View", which included the hit singles "Hold My Hand", "Let Her Cry" and "Only Wanna Be With You". Through the popularity of their grassroots sound, a healthy buzz, and well made music videos, their album went to number one and sold a mind-blowing fifteen million copies in the US alone. From this international sensation, the band toured stadiums and arenas allover the world.

In 1996, Darius and the band released the album "Fairweather Johnson", which went double-platinum in the US, selling more than two million copies. Consequently, Darius and the band hit the road, and again toured the world to support this album.

In 1998, Hootie & the Blowfish released their third album "Musical Chairs", and afterward, an exhausted Darius Rucker decided to take a break from the band. After spending ten long years on the road playing rock music to wild crowds, Darius Rucker decided to return to the music of his youth, and make a R&B record.

Darius recorded a solo debut R&B album "The Return of Mongo Slade", which was slated for release in the summer of 2001, however, due to contractual conflicts with his label Atlantic Records, this album was never distributed. In 2002, now signed to Hidden Beach Recordings, Darius finally released his debut R&B solo album "Back to Then", which was produced by Jeffrey "DJ Jazzy Jeff" Townsend, and featured performances with friends and fellow artist like Jill Scott, Snoop Dogg, and Musiq. The 12 song album included the singles "Sleeping in My Bed", featuring Snoop Dogg, and a moving tribute to his late mother Carolyn, with the re-make of Al Green's "I'm Glad You're Mine". It's been said that, this was the album Darius Rucker always wanted to make. His solo career short lived, Darius returned to the gig that paid the bills, fronting the multi-platinum Hootie & the Blowfish.

As the singer of Hootie & the Blowfish, one of the most commercially successful adult contemporary groups of modern times, Darius Rucker changed the face of mainstream music in the 1990s, selling over 20-million albums worldwide. With class and dignity, Darius has punctuated an already stellar career with a respectful return to his childhood influences. His cool deep voice, and mild rhythmic sound, made Darius Rucker a musical superstar, and a contemporary Rock 'N Roll Hero!

(sources: dariusrucker.com, rollingstone.com, VH1.com, MTV.com)

DIONNE FARRIS

(Born: in 1969, Bordentown, New Jersey)

Born Dionne Yvette Farris in Bordentown, New Jersey, Dionne grew up with a love of singing and dancing. Dionne began her singing career in her high school choir, performing at school functions and at local theaters in Bordentown, where she eventually starred in a production of the musical "Annie". Later, Dionne would join the female vocal group "Onyx", and begin performing in the competitive New York club scene.

Later, young Dionne Farris moved to Atlanta, and began dating Rasa Don, the drummer of the Hip-Hop group "Arrested Development". Dionne began singing with the group, but was never an official member of Arrested Development.

In 1993, Arrested Development had a major hit with the single "Tennessee". However, after the ensuing tour and a Grammy win in 1994, bandleader Speech, Rasa Don, and the rest of Arrested Development summarily disowned Dionne.

In the summer of 1994, with courage and resolve, the now solo Dionne Farris released her own debut album "Wild Seed Wild Flower" on the Sony Records, which included the hit single "I Know", and the equally powerful single "Passion". Dionne spent the rest of the following year touring both alternative/rock and urban/R&B clubs, and made a memorable appearance on "Saturday Night Live". Also included on Dionne's album were the singles "Stop to Think", written by Lenny Kravitz, a moving track in support of victims of physical abuse, "Don't Ever Touch Me (Again)", and a powerful re-make the Beatles' "Blackbird".

Dionne Farris made a powerful mark in Hip-Hop and Alternative Rock. Her smooth and beautiful voice, dances magically over powerfully driven music, like a gleaming rainbow on the edge of a thunder storm. She has accomplished a feat that few have been successful at, Dionne Farris gracefully crossed over from Hip-Hop Princess, to Rock 'N Roll Hero!

(sources: rollingstone.com, VH1.com, MTV.com)

LAURYN HILL

(Born: May 26, 1975, South Orange, New Jersey)

Lauryn Hill was raised in South Orange, New Jersey, where her mother was a high school English teacher and her father a computer programmer. A noticeably intelligent and talented child, Lauryn spent her youth singing along to her parents' record collection, and by the age of 13 she was singing "Who's Lovin' You" on "Showtime at the Apollo", nationally televised from New York.

Soon after, and encouraged by her parents, Lauryn began acting, and earned minor roles on TV shows like the daytime soap "As the World Turns" and in movies like "Sister Act II" with Whoopie Goldberg.

Also at the age of 13, Lauryn Hill began working with the Fugees Wyclef Jean, and Prakazrel "Pras" Michael. But this musical association was often interrupted by both the acting gigs, and later, her acceptance to Columbia University. But eventually Lauryn and the Fugees would begin performing seriously together, and after developing a following on the east coast the Fugees released their debut album "Blunted on Reality", which unfortunately didn't do very well. However, their next album "The Score", which included the mega hit re-make of the Roberta Flack's 1970s hit "Killing Me Softly", catapulted The Score and the Fugees to multi-platinum superstar status.

Lauryn Hill and the Fugees achieved international acclaim, celebrity, and mega financial success. After touring and performing in support of The Score, Lauryn became pregnant, and gave birth to her son Zion, with husband Rohan Marley, son of the late great reggae superstar Bob Marley. The birth of Lauryn's son Zion, inspired her to record a solo album. Now committed to doing her own thing, Lauryn went to a recording studio in New York, and then to Jamaica, where she recorded in the sacred studios of the Bob Marley Museum. Lauryn wrote, arranged and produced just about every track on the album.

In 1998, Lauryn Hill released her solo debut album "The Miseducation of Lauryn Hill", which successfully integrating rap, soul, R&B and reggae into a super successful mixture of musical brilliance. The album included the hit single "Doo Wop (That Thing)", and a blistering host of other mega powerful tracks, displaying Lauryn's musical and lyrical genius.

As The Miseducation of Lauryn Hill began a long reign on the album and singles charts, Lauryn Hill herself was becoming wildly popular as a solo artist, featured on music video channels, and all over the international print media. By the end of the year, the album topped almost every major music chart worldwide, and Lauryn Hill was credited for bringing Hip-Hop vocals into the modern music mainstream.

Lauryn Hill's success was most significantly culminated at the 1999 Grammy awards, where she won five Grammy award trophies from her eleven nominations, including Album of the Year, Best New Artist, Best Female R&B Vocal Performance, Best R&B Song, and Best R&B Album. In the wake of Lauryn's stellar success, she launched a highly praised national tour with Outkast, and Busta Rhymes.

Since, her overwhelming 1999 success, Lauryn Hill has released excellent music that further shows her commitment to quality and freedom in her musical expression. Lauryn Hill is a spiritual, conscientious, and lyrical inspiration to all that hear her music, and to her millions of loving admirers and fans, Lauryn Hill is a Rock 'N Roll Hero and Mega Star.

(sources: artandculture.com, rollingstone.com, VH1.com, MTV.com,, livedaily.cit ysearch.com)

ME'SHELL NDEGE'OCELLO

Pronounced N-day-gay-O-chello, which means "free like a bird", in Swahili   (Born in 1969, US Military Base, Berlin, Germany)

Born Michelle Johnson on a US military base in Berlin, Germany, Me'Shell spent the first few years of her life in Germany, where her father was stationed, and played jazz saxophone. In the early 1970s, Me'Shell's family moved to Virginia, and as a young girl Me'Shell showed a keen interest in music. As a teenager, Me'Shell began to play regularly on the Washington, D.C. club scene, and was accepted into the jazz program at the Duke Ellington School of the Arts, and after that, at Howard University.

At an early age, Me'Shell was an accomplished well-known bass player, who had recorded with jazz artists Steve Coleman, Caron Wheeler, Lenny White, Toshinobu Kubota, and Toshi Reagon. She was also the musical director for Arrested Development's performance on "Saturday Night Live". Notably, Me'Shell was one of the few bassists invited to audition for Living Colour, after the departure of original bassists Muzz Skillings.

In the late 1980s, Me'Shell played with Little Bennie and the Masters and Rare Essence, and in 1990, she won three Washington Area Music Awards. Seeking to be closer to the international music scene, Me'Shell moved to New York in the early 1990s and was commissioned by the executor of the Jimi Hendrix estate to do her versions of Jimi's songs from their catalog.

Me'Shell became very popular on the New York music scene and was offered deals by Prince's Paisley Park Records, Warner Bros. Records and Madonna's Maverick Records. Eventually, Me'Shell signed to Maverick, because the label was new and she would be given the artistic freedom to produce her album her way.

In 1994, Me'Shell Ndege'Ocello released her debut album "Plantation Lullabies", which included the singles and videos "I'm Diggin' You (Like An Old Soul Record)" and "If That's Your Boyfriend (He Wasn't Last Night)". The album received critical international acclaim, and showed the record-buying world, what the musical world already knew:Me'Shell Ndege'Ocello was an incredible talent to be reckoned with. Also that same year, Me'Shell, recorded and starred in the video with John Melloncamp, for his hit re-make of Van Morrison's "Wild Night".

That next year, Me'Shell received four Grammy nominations for Best R&B album, Best R&B Song, Best R&B Vocal Performance Female, and Best Pop Vocal Collaboration with John Melloncamp on Wild Night.

Before recording her next solo album, Me'Shell took time to collaborate with Chaka Khan on the single "Never Miss the Water", as well as writing songs for the movies "White Man's Burden" and "Money Talks". Me'Shell also wrote and recorded material for the multi-artist release "Ain't Nothin' But a She Thang" and the "Lilith Fair Vol. 3" recordings.

In 1996, Me'Shell Ndege'Ocello was honored with the Best Bass Player Award at the Gibson Guitar Awards. Later in 1996, Me'Shell released her second solo album "Peace Beyond Passion", which included eleven self-written songs plus a re-make of Bill Withers "Who Is He and What Is He To You". The album's material was introspectively powerful, and included songs like "The Way", "Deuteronomy: Niggerman", "Ecclesiastes: Free My Heart", "A Tear and A Smile", and "Leviticus: Faggot".

For this incredible album, Me'Shell enlisted a whose who of powerhouse studio musicians, including Joshua Redman on saxophone,

Billy Preston on organ, Wendy Melvoin (of Prince) on guitar, Wah Wah Watson (of Marvin Gaye and Barry White) and arranger Paul Riser, who arranged for the Temptations in the early 1970s.

In 1999, Me'Shell released her third solo album "Bitter", which included the single "Girlfriend", a collaboration with Queen Pen. In 2002, Me'Shell Ndege'Ocello released her fourth album "Cookie: The anthropological mixtape".

Me'Shell Ndege'Ocello is a multi-talented bassist, singer, songwriter and producer who has garnished the respect of the music industry, musicians, and millions of fans alike. Me'Shell is a little woman with a big heart, who has earned the respect of her peers, and the adoration of all who have ever heard her music, and appreciate the importance of this modern day Rock 'N Roll Hero.

(sources: allmusic.com, mavrickrc.com, rollingstone.com, VH1.com)

BEN HARPER

(Born: October 28, 1969, Inland Empire, California)

Benjamin Charles Harper was born and raised in the Inland Empire, east of Los Angeles, California. Ben Harper grew up surrounded by music, his father was a percussionist, his mother a guitarist and singer, who listened to wide range of music. Ben's grandparents had the Folk Music Center where young Ben grew up exposed to a wondrous collection of musical instruments. It was in his grandparents shop that Ben was introduced to his signature instrument, a 1920's Hawaiian lap slide guitar named after its creator, "Weissenborn". Ben's guitar features a fretless hollow neck, and has a classic tone and wonderful sustain.

Ben Harper started playing guitar as a child, and later began performing regularly as a teenager. Ben's musical career got a boost when he was seen playing along side Taj Mahal, and as a result, Ben scored a record deal with Virgin Records in 1992.

In 1994, Ben Harper released his debut album "Welcome to the Cruel World" which included the singles "Don't Take That Attitude to Your Grave" and "Like A King", a song about the dream Martin Luther King envisioned and the ironic nightmare of Rodney King's beating. The album earned critical acclaim for it's powerful performances and it's intelligent lyrical content.

During the 1990s, Ben Harper toured consistently and cultivated a loyal cult following. In 1995, Ben released his second album "Fight For Your Mind", which was considered a politically heavy and strong sophomore effort. "Fight For Your Mind" included the musically powerful single "God Fearing Man", which featured Ben performing some excitingly aggressive slide-guitar work. In 1998, Ben Harper released his third album "The Will to Live", which featured Ben's supporting band the "Innocent Criminals", and became hugely popular at college and adult alternative radio. This third album was recorded over two years of touring in support of 'Fight for Your Mind', and has a distinctly collaborative energy.

Ben Harper and the Innocent Criminals' live shows, are musical spectacles. Ben performs both seated and standing, blisteringly strumming and stroking his guitar, while his band lays down a solidly brilliant foundation for Ben's acrobatics. Ben Harper and the Innocent Criminals put on an amazing live show.

In 1999, Ben Harper and The Innocent Criminals released the album "Burn To Shine", which includes the singles "Suzie Blue", "Steal My Kisses" and "Beloved One". In addition to recording his own material, Ben Harper has built a strong reputation recording with other artists including the late John Lee Hooker. In 2002, Ben enjoyed a major radio hit playing slide guitar on the Jack Johnson single "Flake".

Though he has never had a hit album, Ben Harper's body of work has sold consistently and he circles the world touring and performing in front of thousands of people at a time. Ben Harper and his band the Innocent Criminals continue to produce real music, for real people, and that makes Ben Harper a Rock 'N Roll Hero!

(sources: bonnaroo.com, bandhunt.com, newrootsonline.org, VH1.com)

ALANA DAVIS

(Born in 1974, New York, New York)

Alana Davis was born and raised in Greenwich Village, New York, the daughter of jazz pianist Walter Davis, Jr. and vocalist Annamarie Schofield. Alana started playing guitar as a teenager, and would sit on her bed writing and playing her guitar for hours on end. After briefly attending New York's Mohawk Community College, Alana decided to go into music professionally.

Thanks to a demo that was received by an artist relations executive, at 21, Alana Davis signed a record deal with Elektra Records, and began writing songs for her debut album. The first song she wrote was the title track "Blame it on Me", a "Don't call me, I'll call you!", message to an ex-love.

In 1997, Alana Davis released her debut album "Blame It On Me", which included the singles "Crazy", "Love & Pride", and the hit single "32 Flavors", written by indy sensation Ani Di Franco. The album won worldwide critical acclaim and Time magazine even picked it as one of the year's five best albums. Alana spent the next two years touring extensively in support of Blame It On Me, including dates on the Lilith Fair tour, and the HORDE festival tour.

In 2001, Alana released her second album "Fortune Cookies", which featured eleven beautifully performed songs, and included the single, "I Want You", written by Third Eye Blind's Stephen Jenkins. Later that same year, Alana wrote and recorded the single "I Am Free", which was featured in an American Express advertising campaign.

Alana again toured tirelessly in support of her second album, performing wonderful solo acoustic shows in clubs, and small concert halls, and playing with her band, supporting groups like rock legends Jethro Tull, in arenas.

Alana Davis is a stellar example of talent, vision and beauty. She has a sexy and wondrous gift, and she shares it in song wherever she performs, making Alana Davis a modern day Rock 'N Roll Hero!

(sources: wma.com, aol.com, alanadavis.com, alanadavis.org, VH1.com)

MACY GRAY

(Born: September 9, 1970, Canton, Ohio)

Born Natalie McIntyre in Canton, Ohio, Macy (Natalie) was a quiet child who studied classical piano for seven years. As a youth, Macy's affinity for music was obvious, but when she was little, she had a unique sounding voice, and when she talked, other kids would make fun of her. So, young Macy stopped talking, and everybody thought she was shy, but she was just self-conscious about her voice.

Later, moving to Southern California, Macy was a student in the screenwriting program at the University of Southern California, when she wrote some lyrics as a favor for some musician friends. When it came time to record the songs, the singer didn't show up, so Macy sang instead. The jazzy demo circulated in the Los Angeles area, and the positive feedback it received focused on Macy's brilliant vocal performance. So, Macy joined the band full-time and began playing relatively high-paying gigs.

Macy was making good money singing jazz standards and really enjoying herself. Consequently, and due to her reputation as a sought-after Jazz session vocalist, in 1998, Macy Gray was signed to Epic records and was in the studio two months later, recording her debut album. In 1999, Macy Gray released her debut album "On How Life Is", which had already undergone a seven month promotional campaign and included the hit singles "Do Something", "I Try", "Why Didn't You Call Me", and "Still". Macy set out on a grueling world tour to promote her album, performing in every major city nationally and internationally.

"On How Life Is" earned Macy respect and recognition among her peers and admirers alike. With her rigorous tour schedule, videos, television appearances, and print media coverage, Macy Gray made a serious name for herself worldwide, and promoted her debut album to triple-platinum status.

In 2001, Macy released her sophomore album, "The Id", which included the single "Sweet Baby". Also, in 2001, Macy appeared in the Academy Award Winning film "Training Day", holding her own while trading lines with powerhouse actor and double-Oscar Award Winner Denzel Washington.

Macy Gray is a unique and beautifully talented singer and performer. She has made a great impact on modern music in her young recording career. Macy has the kind of focus and vision that will enable her to make great strides in the music industry. Macy Gray is impressively well on her way to securing her musical legacy as a Rock 'N Roll Hero!

(sources: MTV.com, VH1.com, rollingstone.com, divastation.com)

HIP-HOP ARTISTS: THE NEW ROCKSTARS

In the New Millennium, African American Hip-Hop/Rap Artists have undeniably become the new Pop-Culture Icons and Rock Stars. Multi-million dollar recording and video budgets, personalized clothing lines, fleets of private jets, limousines, entourages and servant-filled mansions have become the standard set by these New Millennium Music Moguls.

Wealthy high-profile Hip-Hop artist like P. Diddy, Jay-Z, Master-P, and Missy Elliot, are internationally celebrated examples of the overwhelming influence of African American Hip-Hop/Rap artists on corporate, mainstream, middle, and urban America.

Even legendary departed Rap Artists, like the late great Tupac Shakur and The Notorious B.I.G., have had an undisputedly powerful impact on modern music and mainstream culture. I believe that we've only scratched the surface of Hip-Hop's influence on popular culture, both nationally and internationally.

CONCLUSION

The influence and contributions of African Americans in Rock music culture is so powerful and profound that it now sounds absurd to have ever separated or segregated Pop music genres. But, reflectively, segregation was an American mainstay in the early 1950s, when the African American Blues, Gospel, and Jazz artists were creating the music that would become Rock 'N Roll.

Disappointingly, after more than fifty years of perceived social progress, and at the dawn of a new millennium full of the promises of political correctness, renewed social justice, legislated equal opportunity, and ultra-vigilant civil rights protection, the musical entertainment industry still practices an overt form of categorical and racial segregation in musical genres.

Some might argue that it's this very separation that creates an inherent safe-haven in which African American music can survive and thrive, without having to openly compete on the same album and singles charts as mainstream European American Pop acts and artists. Some might consider this the music industry's version of "Affirmative Action". It could also be argued that the segregation of R&B and Rock, Pop, and Alternative, is just as reasonable as the separation of Jazz, Classical, and Adult Contemporary.

All arguments acknowledged, it is an undisputed fact that African American artists, musicians, and singers, established an unbroken line of influence that runs straight through the heart of American music, and is historically validated as the very Soul Of Rock 'N Roll.

HONORABLE MENTION

Albert Collins
Albert King
Angie Stone
Ashford & Simpson
Baby Face
Ben E. King
Billy Cox
Billy Stewart
Brownie McGee
Buddy Guy
Buddy Miles
Carlos Mikell
Chaka Khan
Cherokee
Chubby Checker
Cree Summer
D'Angelo
Dionne Warwick
Donna Summer
Eric McFadden
Erykah Badu
Fats Domino
Frankie Lymon
Gladys Knight
Gloria Gainer
Graham Central Station
Gregg Howe
Harvey
Herbie Hancock
Imij
India Arie
James Blood Ulmer
Jay King
Jeffrey Gaines
Jill Scott
Joe Public
Johnny Nash
Katon De Pena
Kool & The Gang
Lajon Witherspoon

Latoya Jackson
Lightnin' Hopkins
Marcus Miller
Mary Wells
Matt "Guitar" Murphy
Maxwell
Michael Franti
Musiq
Narada M. Walden
Nat King Cole
Orlando X
Patti LaBelle
PMS
Ray Parker Jr.
Rebe Jackson
Robert Johnson
Rocky George
Rosie Gaines
Sammy Davis Jr.
Saul "Slash" Hudson
T.M. Stevens
The Black Rock Coalition
The Bus Boys
The Debarge Family
The Four Tops
The Funk Brothers
The Neville Brothers
The O'Jays
The Pointer Sisters
The Roots
The Sisters Sledge
The Stylistics
The Time
Tiran Porter
Tom Morello
Tory Ruffin
Vanity
War
William Duvall
Wilson Pickett

There are many other wondrously important performers who were not mentioned, but have had a unique and powerful impact on the history of American Rock 'N Roll and Rock music internationally. Specifically, this book was written to show a linear progression of influence by African American musicians by generation and rock genre.

"To all of the artists not mentioned, I give homage and respect."

J.Othello